GONDWANA
and Other Poems

ALSO BY NATHANIEL TARN

POETRY

The Persephones, 1974, (rewritten) 2008, 2016
The Beautiful Contradictions, 1969, 2013
Ins and Outs of the Forest Rivers, 2008 • Avia, 2008
Recollections of Being, 2004 • Selected Poems: 1950–2000, 2002
Three Letters from the City: the St. Petersburg Poems, 2001
The Architextures, 2000 • The Architextures 1–7, 1999
A Multitude of One (editor: poems by Natasha Tarn), 1994
Flying the Body, 1993
Caja del Río, 1993 • The Army Has Announced that Body Bags…, 1992
Home One, 1990 • Seeing America First, 1989
The Mothers of Matagalpa, 1989 • At the Western Gates, 1985
The Desert Mothers, 1984 • Weekends in Mexico, 1982
The Land Songs, 1981 • Atitlán/Alashka (w. Janet Rodney), 1979
Birdscapes, with Seaside, 1978
The Forest: from Alashka (w. Janet Rodney), 1978
The Ground of Our Great Admiration of Nature: from Alashka (w. Janet Rodney), 1977
The Microcosm, 1977 • The House of Leaves, 1976
Lyrics for the Bride of God, 1975 • Section: The Artemision, 1973
A Nowhere for Vallejo, 1971 • The Silence, 1969 • October, 1969
Where Babylon Ends, 1969
Selection: Penguin Modern Poets, 7, 1965 • Thirteen for Bled, 1965
Old Savage/Young City, 1964

TRANSLATIONS

The Penguin Neruda, 1975 • The Rabinal Achi, Act 4, 1973
Con Cuba, 1969 • Stelae (Segalen), 1969 • Selected Poems (Neruda), 1968
The Heights of Macchu Picchu (Neruda), 1966

PROSE

The Embattled Lyric: Essays & Conversations in Poetics & Anthropology, 2007
Scandals in the House of Birds: Shamans & Priests on Lake Atitlán, 1998
Views from the Weaving Mountain: Selected Essays in Poetics & Anthropology, 1991

GONDWANA
and Other Poems

Nathaniel Tarn

A NEW DIRECTIONS PAPERBOOK ORIGINAL

Thanks to the editors of the following magazines and anthologies in which some of these poems first appeared: *Contemporary Poetry: Nature and Myth* (Corbel Stone Press, 2017), *Fact-Simile, Hambone, Jacket, Lute & Drum, New American Literature, Poetry Salzburg, Resist Much / Obey Little: Inaugural Poems to the Resistance* (Spuyten Duyvil: Dispatches Editions, 2017), *Seedings* (Duration Press), *Stonecutter, TriQuarterly*, and *Zen Monster.*

Thanks also to Christopher Benson at The Fisher Press in Santa Fe, New Mexico, for first publishing "Il Piccolo Paradiso" in an edition of twenty copies with his photographs in 2015.

Manufactured in the United States of America
New Directions Books are printed on acid-free paper
First published as a New Directions Paperbook (NDP1381) in 2017
Design by Eileen Baumgartner

Library of Congress Cataloging-in-Publication Data
Names: Tarn, Nathaniel, author.
Title: Gondwana & other poems / Nathaniel Tarn.
Description: New York, NY : New Directions Publishing, 2017.
Identifiers: LCCN 2017009769 | ISBN 9780811225021 (alk. paper)
Classification: LCC PS3570.A635 A6 2017 | DDC 811/.54—dc23
LC record available at https://lccn.loc.gov/2017009769

10 9 8 7 6 5 4 3 2 1

New Directions Books are published for James Laughlin
by New Directions Publishing Corporation
80 Eighth Avenue, New York 10011

ndbooks.com

For Janet Rodney

CONTENTS

ONE: GONDWANA

Gondwana   3

TWO: THE STAIRS AT FEZ

Birds: Bosque del Apache, NM   15
Romancero (Daoist)   17
Occupy Santa Fe, Her Afghan Night   18
Fact Lines   20
Nerval's Maidenhair (Fern)   22
In Love with the Queen of Amherst   24
Old Friedrich, Sils-Maria, 06.30.1928   28
The Stairs at Fez   31

THREE: IL PICCOLO PARADISO

Il Piccolo   39
In a State   41
Reading through Sleep   43
Moment   45
A Spider's Prisoner   47
Veil   49
The Price   51
Angels   53
Thing   55
Maya   56
Books Falling   58
Anomia   59
Sleeper   61
Arrival   62
Heart. Mode Recall   64
Definition   66

FOUR: FIGHTER PILOTS

(Eurydice, Sr. Lt., Rising in Re & To: Orpheus, Capt., Setting)   69

FIVE: EXITUS GENERIS HUMANI

E. G. H., I
1. Visitor   85
2. Torture: A Rage   87
3. Vital Signs (the Poltergeist)   89
4. Burial Mound North   91
5. *Divas*   93
6. Lungs Floating, Slick   95
7. Mammoth Excretions   97
8. Cold Unmistakable   99
9. Laughing, Singing, Praying Trees   101

E. G. H., II
A. As if Philosophy   103
B. Responses   105
C. Hootless at Heart & Flying   107

E. G. H., III
I. Paris Old   108
II. The Homer   109
III. The Guest   110
IV. For MacDiarmid of that Ilk / The Passing   112
V. The Olson Thing / Nihil Obstat? / The Passing   114
VI. The Promises   116
VII. Individuality, Solitudes   117
VIII. Recently Assayed   119
IX. The Longing & Desire for Justice Condign to the End:
   A Preseason Sale   121
X. *Die Unendlichen*   123

ONE: GONDWANA

Incedo per ignes

GONDWANA

ψυχὰς ἔχοντες κυμάτων ἐν ἀγκάλαις

Their lives / Held in the arms / Of the waves.
—Archilochus, *Carmina Archilochi*, no. 174,
tr. by Guy Davenport

Here, now, as ever, going out again
from *Finis Terre*, final of earth, or
"end of world" they call it here,
consumption left behind.
Earth fragments—first the big islands
cannot be told from earth, then
smaller and smaller islands among
their channels, trees grabbing soil
with weaker roots, until all's rock where
unimagination starts, where
tempests flare around dread Horn.
Last inhabitants' blazing canoes
expose their nakedness to last explorers.
This plot begins and ends with past.
But what we name the future follows on.

Earth sinks into mind
sea being mind of earth
in constant movement, constant fretting,
endlessly leaping from thoughts to thought,
waves rolling in from the planet's belt
greet each other as far-flung kin.
Deep in each trough, thriving unseen,
huge beast obsessions: small
secret beasts; beasts with invading arms
long as your most fearsome nightmares.

###

Sea lifts its swell into whales.
Smallest speck of foam
is a bird paddling along a wave crest
almost invisible in search of upturn.
How fathomless this is!
What is going on down there,
how far do you drop in the abyss
before feeling ground,
before a basis offers rest again, foothold,
security? Meantime ghosts
of the dead at sea:
circling weather's homeless
tantalize waves with wing tips
as they go round the endless dip and rise,
cruising cool air. May not alight for years.

                                              ###

Toward center,
center of center,
where earth-mind turns solid,
whereto a single bird
may fly per annum, attracted by
some odor, some phantom odor,
while most, standing, in glossy caucuses
hold a circumference for access to the sea.
A silence there hard to believe, a hazeless,
dustless air when in the clear: a spot
on the farther side of knowledge
from which all other points are North.
Where is your "epilepsy" West,
your "wisdom" East when everything
flies you away from known dimensions
into the stillness? This is no crossing
from a river's bank to its other side, but
lack of movement absolute,
total attention
to a deliberate deliverance.
The orb has turned all diamond.

###

Birds melting in and out of waves
caressing tip with tip but never touching them,
bird, beast, eyes peeking out—a quick
look-see and gone again. Ice
opens, closes. Length-wise
black lines of sleeping animal,
height-wise gray lines of wary bird:
those that fly in sea,
those that swim in air.
Some that flash snow and bathe in snow
white as the ivory light
roll on their backs in snow at times:
black eye, black beak, black foot
signal a presence over white on white.
Some that are checkerboards in black
and white, set your cold eyes to shivering.

###

The days stretch into years or seem to
for all the world has told us of itself.
Anything new revealed?
High mirrored in a low
has been known forever.
Low rising to a high stays moot.
Sun floating here in mid-floe mist
unwilling to climb or fall,
unfurls a panoply of colors.
Mythical grass flashes its green.
Phenomena can all forget forgetting
except the huge electric sea.
Now you imagine days,
similar to days,
days after days uncountable,
days cannot be outnumbered
by any calendric art. They are
a single day—or very few you'll swear

by lights of the old stars,
and, while innumerable in fact,
these cannot be distinguished.

###

Domain pitches and rolls:
hearts out of throats,
muscles tightened to lock in breath,
backs slamming up against the bulwarks,
"one hand to ship," one to your life.
A very tender roll,
soft yet relentless, moving us
from incarnation to incarnation.
You would not think such gentle motion,
a whisper in earth's circles,
could leave even your mind unbalanced.
But mind escapes like bird into mist.
Perhaps this is your coffin
propelled into white fire
out of one universe into another.

###

As you reach the great white
peak of the single color,
emotions have been draining
out of your lives.
Naked you go into this continent
in endless search of cleanliness,
exiled imagination's only host,
until imagination rots.
Catchword "reality" assumes a meaning now,
breath suddenly leaps fast,
distance-devouring clarity
brings all the secrets of the continent
close up against your eyes.
This is the moment of desisting
from human will. Whatever flares:

slide along sea lanes, whitewash away.
With the... no, *not* the fear of dying, no—
but an immeasurable depth of sadness
for having such a trifling time
to deal with the one hundred thousand things.

[Far back in another dimension,
far as you cannot remember,
all wenches dead, the culture petrified,
dance music curls on flowing flowers:
freeze to the ice of heartbreak and there *is* such.
Your body may sense it as you move
and step it—yet it's only dream.
Despised, acclaimed, despised again through over-
hype, you cannot hear it here—
engulfed by silence and immense white air.]

They said back then
there was a frozen continent
in those high latitudes encircles globe.
Are you moving toward it?
Sea overwhelms all distance,
spreads out beyond its cup into space—
there is no other explanation
for how long you have been moving
toward no destination.
You can imagine white
drawing in your colors,
all body differentiae,
until you walk as a ghost,
as someone who has crossed
a limit on no map.
It can be described also
as having crossed to the other side
whether this be a river

or earth-girdler's self. But,
as you know, there is no crossing.

###

Is it possible to be overwhelmed
by landscape? Yes. Engulfed? Yes.
Sparagmatized? Broken into shards? Yes.
Sun so blinding in ice facets
borders fade and you enter
what hunters have known for centuries:
silence of silence. No silence on known
ground outsilences this silence.
What is an individual
so spread over so many miles
eyes can't encompass them?
Eventually you'll wear
pelts of all animals
you have come far, at such
expenditure of energy,
to witness. Nothing is heard
of the alleged known-world
for however long a time
you come to donate here.

###

Above leviathan's songs
can be sensed in your trembling limbs
laments of captive ships,
locked, crushed and,
piece by piece, delivered to the ice—
their dislocated bodies
berthed into other waters than their own.
Everything brought from out. Outside
dissolves. Eyes shut,
the creatures never seem to need to see,
eyes free are globes of melted ice.
Yourself in that beast's pelt

rests economically on a blue berg,
gazes a moment at the undocumented,
(zodiac pass by!), eyes close again.
Blindly you lead the blind through paradise.

Cruising up channel,
whose sides seem to fall in on you,
held in a block of time:
it could be a cage—but these are walls not bars.
No height can be ascribed to the walls.
As in a code revealed,
white veins blink through black stone,
damming your eyesight.
Even on cloudless days, rocks climb on up,
so measureless, they will outlast your sight
and terminate it.

Where the initiating bang
unpacked imagination's jar
emptying it once and for all,
the jar of one named as
all-gifts, all-giving:
how falsely named!
A small meteorite
from our uncounted universes
slammed here, name cruelty.
No thing, no person spared.
Truth that we are at any moment
in any time, in any place,
less than a hair away
from ultimate disaster.
Close as the wrist watch on your
wrist. In this possession,
this epilepsy if you will,
mind unfurls

(like a great banner of its own freedom
while white raises balloons—
the weather's breasts)
and will accept its fate.
Of all the gifts, kept by an after-thought
hope only held the jar.

###

Coming back to your life, your everyday,
the one they call with relish "normal"
and how you hate it!
Through days of outrageous storm,
ship lolling like a drunk, navel
in throat, brine coating mouth
with its obscene concoctions.
Obsession slides, slits waves.
Not allowed to move
of your own volition
but pushed this way and that discretionless,
day after day though the roll lasts soft
and would hardly seem fierce enough
to move a marble from child to child.

###

Returned from a now known sphere
for the first time completely, and thus
"at home," the sphere can never be itself
once more. Done to itself in the meantime?
You cannot fathom. You have not heard
"the news" for all the time away. Suddenly
you realize you may not hear "the news"
again. This race in its inhuman sadness
calls itself human still—but holds
no further value. It no longer serves
as yardstick for comparisons.
The robot's been switched on.
You have seen creatures who, full versed

in every ethic, act with such spontaneity
that they will never *judge*. You have been
gathered into Eden yet found it full.
Your body as a ship is now at rest,
yet there's no berth for you to sleep in.

###

Purchased by sea
you will never walk the same.
Lines will never be straight but curve
continually in an attempt at straight.
This beloved earth loses its strength.
Drugs drown ultimate coral colors;
krill devolves into mud; animal
flesh, slashed open to its innards,
washes to liquid pinks: diluted wine.
Shit pink, you stink among dry corpses,
your guts groped at by scavengers.
Much precious ice washes away to sea
never to startle cloud again.
Waves flush out of your pockets,
pant-bottoms, mouths and ears—your
bones reclaimed in full by foam.

###

The tallest universal star, cloud-born,
earth raised beyond the highest suns:
one single goddess for humankind,
one sole divinity for our necessity:
salvage no other! worship no other,
turning all ritual to work!
She walking out from loss, dying, dead,
she who obliterates all other gods,
now comes to life again,
now smiling breathes, entices. You
meditate by warm streams while molting—
streams you sang beside as your city perished,

paddle breathlessly instead of flying,
sound like every being except yourself,
experience the ultimate in solitude.
The robot has been terminated.
After some seeming centuries
the northward-pointing cross collapses,
all our directions open free.
Your heart, once given to embalmers
in the empires of *Finis Terre*,
suddenly homes with you to mate again.

Antarctica, 2008

TWO: THE STAIRS AT FEZ

BIRDS: BOSQUE DEL APACHE, NM

Azure deploys its falcons, eagles, hawks
watching from single masts over the lakes,
thousands of geese snow-colored and snow-
stained. Raptors bird also. Mad paparazzi
birders crowd into hide: deck, solid deck.
With giant apparatus, lens clutches, multiple
focus—crowd out a seeming simple but oh
so complex lover hidden at reeds for whom
the light's more precious *ipso facto* than any
image—and, let us say, birthed elsewhere.
From the left screen side (no East in here),
sun rises painfully as if he's somewhat lame,
hauled up out of his depths by all his ances-
tors: that much is needed while this planet
glows. Quiet between goose horns, crane
castanets. All this come down from the far
North. (No Arctic owls know how to sing:
Snow Owl, most silent ghost, delivers up
her mice without a note.) So to what mindless
here where self's at bay for once? Light now
blankets a single body, this only, living, angel,
Earth. To be called "paradise" by those—those
many travel yearly through their lives as to
a sanctuary. (How many sites deserve the name
this name of holy "paradise" birds only know.)

Of light and hush, let's just say quietude, quiet,
invisible clean ice—the stainless kind you can
see through as clean as glass but newly fitted
on eyes that were too blind before, roves over
grasses birds are grazing at—lover is moved
as if by magic without moving. Lifted into the
dawn, who but that watcher waits on, with his birds,
waiting also on waters more and more clamorous:
his birds lift of a sudden before watcher breathes,
they too, unmoving, seeming skim the lakes, then

border bushes, and then the clouds (but clouds invisible in this perfected morning) and on into a (some could call) paradise (here is the word again) so much the word seems to be called for. No Heaven, no such Bird. Only azure... *L'azur, l'azur!*

They pass, clean overhead, larger and larger waxing, dawn light sketches their bodies and devours them. And peace, which "passes understanding," a single instant frightened by birds into the watcher's heart and lodging there, that, yes, can be acknowledged. You lifted us, winged hearts, feeding your simple purposes (that purpose purposive)—we with our complicated demarcations that you never need— whole Earth lifts from a single moment here, the deep, colorless omega, our desert's sense of it. Far down from here, how can we name it? How think of it? Distance fades ever: within no further South.

ROMANCERO (DAOIST)

In memoriam Michel Strickmann, Sinologist

Incredibly, from vertical to horizontal in one
moment—moment as long as some sung pas-
sages in bygone eras from a named purgatory
to a named heaven, the day, turning from tem-
pest to just fine; all louring clouds drowning
earth to smiling sapphire; bronzed landscapes
into emerald; quiescent birds now perpetrating
riots of conjugated melody. Romantic time has
now evolved from patience to consumption. Be-
low the birthplace of the earth K'un-lun, wreath
of black, blond and burnished auras: its mines
await the miner while from blood and lymph he
turns mud into gold and diamonds. Higher than
centrifugal valley: all senses radiating, the birth-
place puckered symbol smiling in its heartland,
twin mountains holding up the planet high above
the centripetal turtle understanding. Higher yet,
those two-way windows giving/receiving open
onto the widest turquoise sky, closing as breath
comes faster, flights of fancy multiply... and mas-
tery of life flowers spreading its seeds with wind-
like laughs. P'eng-lai! Now to go East young man
once more and sunward! Is it not passing brave to
be a king and ride in triumph through Persepolis?

OCCUPY SANTA FE, HER AFGHAN NIGHT

> One Nation ... Under-Educated
> —Bumper sticker

Light hesitates to fix, to position itself
between night's huge twin mammaries
spewing their milk across our universe,
the crusts and ridges of our desert roads.
Halogen lamps housed under cars: our
mices love to nest inside these yes-you-
vees munching at all the wires. Light
spatters land because, downtown, a city,
ignoring where it stops and starts, has
spread unnumbered blocks since a first
visit—but its parameters continue vague.
From air, city can never promise grid or
pattern. Paternalistic copters wink in the
quiet, their blades split angry lightning
followed by some belated thunder. Did
we walk up to the P.O. today to see stars
flying among stripes, make sure we are
secure in a familiar country? Facing the
faces from another desert in some broke,
or else dying, East—a movie!—brought
understanding: "no fear" no longer holds.
We *must* haul ass, get *out*, get "home" if
can be, sand to sand, bury our insolence.
So many dead in previous scrums, sons of
poor Nuevomex! *Vaterland* falters! Never-
theless, it is not reading this—so please
bewilder it! At "Cowgirl Bar," downtown,
company riots in various kitsch modes they
dance their hearts out to. Our rest of town
lies sleeping: a very early town. It dreams
does it? O *Liberal* it thinks itself in the dead
blather passes for language now: the wish
to a good day, a wonderful, a maravillious
day! Prior to sleep, please plot a great com-

bustion. In a sweet dream pick presidential
rats, the stark rat-race obscenity, root of the
whole insane disaster, rot of the loving land,
plant them in ordure, recycled garbage. Throw
hands jointly between boss legs, palm up to
perineum, lift up the old morass, pitch it to fire.

July 2010

FACT LINES

For Jeffrey Yang

Facts. From out wings,
rafters, from under floors,
from windows, doors, from the diminutive
holes mice use to conquer *domus*,
whether of past, present, future, whether
digested, (not), understood, (not), or, well,
so super-parsed, so wondrous comprehended,
thru prisms of documented centuries.

Two feet crossed. Fall asleep. Sensation of two feet
crossed. Wake: and not crossed. Correct determination?
"The immanence of revelation which does not occur"
       of revolution! revolution!

From here to not remembering life led—
Eternal Body of Imagination—
hidden among un-penetrated convolutions
of brain, those jungles. An overwhelming question:
who (who)? what (war)? what (earthquake)? what (disaster)?
and what collapse of the whole goddam race
brings down this broken star of self? Heaviest load
a human bears is how to separate from other humans,
how they stand separate, the lives they lead,
the each in each, each out of each,
the sense of entities precluded from all meeting,
discourse, and all discussion—because of barriers
no flesh can cross, no mind can entertain, no will can move.

In "*the desert of the real*,"
                    indeed we saw the desert,
for seven days and seven nights
                    we knew the desert,
and proved it was impossible to live
                    without the desert.
So thus the messenger, the spy, the winged intelligence
                    in flight up from his ark
brought satisfaction with a desert fate.

Jade: signature of a perfected heaven.
But "*metaphysic of commodity exchange: to never
know with whom we are connected.*" So this the life
that we must lead, loving or (not), conscious or (not),
sounding or (not), down to untutored trenches of the sea—
and resurrected from the sulfur springs,
profound green algae rising from the clefts,
in wave submerged there now—
                    to look up at a distant winter sun?

"*The mind so near itself—it cannot see, distinctly.*"
The mind made a republic you have encompassed:
this huge, immense you see, rotted America
divided from itself,
to be reborn elsewhere:
            perhaps on Mars, perhaps Europa, perhaps Titan.

NERVAL'S MAIDENHAIR (FERN)

Aurelia's

All night devouring the streets of Paris,
as if I'd never left the unforgiving city—
city I thought I'd die of... if I ever left it.
Maidenhair on the desk. Sixty years since
a book was written over these fronds,
out of these very leaves, [face fallen into
them]—they have never evolved, as this
guy has, toward oblivion despite the
stretch of evolution. A fill of sixty years
after such greens hallowed the writing
desk: ready to talk. Between & latterly
they were reviewed along the roadsides
of the emerald Andes. But giant there, so
large you thought one plant could fill a
province. In that southern night, sudden
electric eyes of *hope*, dead all the mean-
time, opened, [opened once only in the
night], [alas for once!] and it was like a
kind of adoration, of recognition—a thing
I had, maybe had had, & lost in the far past?
                                        Aurelia!

But that immense, immeasurable *hope*,
working on down the ages, the everlasting
& immemorial, & seeming indestructible,
timeless apparently but riddled yet with
time—it is a *lie*, no longer living—kept
moving only by men's insanity, aimed at
giving another clearer reason to their lives
than even sun hands down in diamonds &
in gold. She had belonged, no, not to him,
never to him, brightest that shines the dead-
lier, but to the other irretrievably & he could
only yield. And since: the dying bloom of
hope. But he is blind from birth on now: he

cannot use those eyes. Hanging from some lamp-lighting post, gray in the bowels of no city but in a cruel desert. And hardly singing from that lost day forever into this other life.

IN LOVE WITH THE QUEEN OF AMHERST

Courage: three days to Lit. annihilation,
to the Dark Silence, a turning of the Back.

1.

Believing I am in love, in love severe
& lasting, with Dickinson, Miss E.
It's happened very suddenly, almost
in the blink of an eye. So sudden I am
in no ways sure of it—and may not be
for whiles. I think she is the mother of
America: at any rate the first and primal
woman of these States and there has been
no one, inside or outside of her solitude,
in any way to match her. It's also true
that these were not only the first—but
oh the richest days of Nation. My Nation
bloomed in her but has had mighty pain
in fruiting ever since—until our very time.
That's in the way might just have been
expected from out the sovereign force
of that deep primal batch. I say Thoreau,
Whitman, Emerson, Hawthorne, Melville.

2.

But the main thing is that she needs the
making love to. (Some others may have
tried—in no way brilliantly?). Something
her culture and circumstance forbade.
Something Nation ferociously demanded:
Sex as a metaphor for Matriotism. We
are not groping: it is chivalry. Case of
dama dolente and sighing knight? No. So
hard to say she would not have desired it
(rather as in Jane Austen's case with whom

I would also have been o.k. to love or marry.)
They are supposed to have selected art, but
art chose them and no one can determine
how much they could have been, humanly
speaking, satisfied. There seems to be
agreement E. was not "good looking,"
in no way any kind of beauty (much like
Jane) but I cannot agree. She seems to me
exceedingly good looking, most attractive
(I talk of age sixteen—the sweet sixteen
so many fuss about) and I'd have been most
glad to close with her. Why, even now, in
the imagination... can be encompassed. Did
they have showers in those days? It would
have been so good to stand in one with her
and to insert a tongue into each armpit, and
then in other regions, some more intimate.
Whatever's said about her prudence, I find
no reason on this earth why she'd have been
in any way distressed, in any way denying.
But bring on James, the England-lover, a
classic, long-sentenced, superstar of endless
conversation: how long it took to let love
speak (as per our South in *The Bostonians*:
Male fatal arrogance, unbounded, limitless).

3.

Jane's tomb: her family forgot to signify her
pressing claim to fame. The Novels are a mar-
vel, however limited in universal scope,
and a delight. E.D. may be the greatest poet
Nation ever produced and barring none.
Formal invention was not her *forte* as far as our
tastes are concerned—but for that time it was
superior. And her capacity for sudden leaps of
color, astonishment at sudden leaps, the lay
of seasons and of light, astounding capture

of surprise (with seemingly) quietus of
exertion, never can cease to win our absolution.
She is a form of miracle where nothing such,
despite all claims, could ever have been
welcomed to exist. The early gravestone, at the
least, manifests little. Bless you, dear silence.

4.

This is the start, love or no love, of an
enormous solitude. It's no small thing
to turn your back on everything that you
have ever done, or said in praise, or blame,
of any *what* at all pertaining to the world
you'd made your own. Turning your back
is vast advent, leaving you wholly open
to hunger, pain, and thirst—thirst being
for an angel's tongue beyond the boundaries.
Wakings are worst—when implications
home to roost, when consequences home
(oh yes so daintily) to roost, though there is
some strange courage invades the days—
almost as if intolerable burdens were to be
lifted high off the soul and off the back.
That back is an extremely strong, powerful
facet. When enemies consider you done-gone,
plotting on down the bleeding hill—your
back, a traitor to the good, flag, constitu-
tion—those same considerations, with this
so fierce a love for Emily, call down vast
consolation. The back, do not forget, bears
high your arms when the aim is skyward.
All to be knighted, ha, in this "democracy"?
And, since all hope is one, magnanimous,
however many more may share in it: now
that both citizen and nation sink together,
I glory once in this disastrous age, sharing
the bliss with my dear Sister Wife—you

well know who—before dark falls again
over each shattered moment of a day—with
that single exception. Waking to slumber.

OLD FRIEDRICH, SILS-MARIA, 06.30.1928

For P, A, A, I, M, F, B, K, J.

1.

Now to the embraces of the mountains,
high tower ridges naked above the valleys,
rock arms around my life. All dispossessed of
family & friendship, abeyance from disaster.
Was ever more than this... this total isolation
bred into lineage, inheritance, or expectations
regarding futures? Ever a mother?... father?...
siblings? I remember nothing save, rising from
graves, assembling back his limbs, his stature
to my eyes, a man invisible & preternatural
called me to loss. I see the future. And yet
for now, the deep green childhood meadows:
rioting flowers in such profusion no botany
encompasses them all. Moment by moment
on long walks, I re-acquaint myself toward
kind names, their color gradually restored by
this or that re-visit with a childhood moment—
as when, for instance, I had climbed a torrent,
a mighty cataract it seemed to me—my boots
sliding from rock to rock & each rock hosting
a single flower as I now dream this floor. Float-
ing, free of philosophers, historians, artists &
poets, mongrels & mongers of every discipline,
the uncreative, the competently deathly: free of
those whole infernal crowds. Interminable pain
even in a ghost's limbs—but blissfully at work
through pain to guarantee my universe release.

2. (a & b)

A plenitude of orchids—What! orchids outside tropics?
in the blue-green cathedral under the northing iceberg;

skyfulls of flute-blooms, & trombone-gentians lurking
on walls sunk to a planet's crust at the sea's fundament;
among high grasses; larkspur; monk's hood jockeying
as if you walked on sand back home in broiling desert
for open skies; the purple aquilegia reminiscing Rome
as you did, rapt and fiery, through the helling canyons;
the clematis—star of the alps; buttercup gold aflame:
never have human *eyes seen this before, nor ever will*
& globe-plants, hoisting will to power over fellows,
enter the kingdom some may call god—but it is not—
mustard & cress; stonecrop & saxifrage; & artemisia;
not god, but distant ancestors who paled at creatures
clover & potentilla; rose; iris; sunspark; meadow-saffron;
so dangerous they fled in panic to the closest shoreline,
silene & willow-herb; foxglove; snowbell & crowfoot;
& slow, from frightful sinews, teeth, maws & tentacles,
fireweed; myosotis (forget me not); campanula & fern;
shrank & moved on into our arms, legs, uprightness,
yarrow; vetch; daisy; edelweiss—heraldic of the only
deities, i.e. our earthly selves, now worth our trouble...

But always a catastrophe to our own kind, so *nothing
gained us out of that mortal sea.* And rain engulfs the
mountains. Ah! meadows drown! *Here beauty reigned,
beauty* alone, without a menace, only a dream of fields
lives on—like bird-calls heard *where our last, terminal
extinction* fades away. Deep in the misted-over jungles
the race has done exploring: all the land's *mapped out.*
Mostly, the prophesiers say, our species won't survive.

3.

My room as simple as it could be, not one item
of furniture *de trop*, the writing tools on desk as
limited as possible to clarify a mind's intent. I
work against a head in shards, eyes almost blind,
vomit in throat at any moment, the fall & sink of
nausea, the dizziness, the need unquestioned for

crashing head to floor and float till I can parse
again. My room a box among these wildernesses,
a dream, within a sleep, within a death—*that* one
to come v. soon is my belief—but "positive!" as
a last flag of this my nothingness. And death a box
within this body, room within room and far too
deep for anger. I have discredited all the external
causes and unsubscribed mankind to all divinities,
all outside help for the atrocious misery in which it
ferments. On the behalf of spirits, mankind has
wasted worlds that it was given, continues trashing
them and will go on *idem* until they & mankind
enjoy their death together. "Consider a lily of the
field" an enemy pronounced: I love my frenemies!
Consider it indeed and all the tribes of plants &
all the tribes of animals that feed on them, consider
the whole tree, the central pillar: do we not pull it
down? To this proposal I bend my life here, all
my activity. Had we not wasted Eden, all space &
so much of our time, could we not have prevented
more disasters, worked out more cures, dominated
hell, returned man/woman back into their garden,
assuaged the doubts & terrors of our only goddess
—if there be need of gods—this lonesome Earth?

THE STAIRS AT FEZ

For Anna Della Subin & Hussein Omar

Perché non spero tornare giammai nella città delle belleze
eccomi di ritorno in me stessa. Perché non spero mai ritrovare
me stessa, eccomi di ritorno fra delle mura. Le mura pesanti
e ignare rinchiudono il prigioniero.

Because I do not hope ever to return to the city of beauty
here I am back inside myself. Because I do not hope ever to find
myself again, here I am back between walls. Heavy and dull
walls shut in the prisoner.

—Amelia Rosselli, *Variazioni Belliche*,
tr. by Lucia Re & Paul Vangelisti

1.

Stairs, the impossible stairs,
the almost impossible stairs,
killer, leg-breaking stairs,
whole legs cramping at night,
mounting into the privacies.
Shop: high-piled treasures,
brought from the distant mountains
High Atlas say—for sullen sale
to infidels in such strange clothes
as monkeys wore once mayhap
at Andaluz for work in circuses.
"I sell you these blankets
made of fine camel hair: young camel
in this band, old camel in this one
and with a simple badge,
black tribal badge, the fine tattoo
worn by our women between breasts
and maybe further down. You buy
two rugs now for the price of one,
you take them home, out from our

family, from the High Atlas,
ruled by the lords of snow—
now you have drunk this mint with us
from the bleak mountains on a blind horizon."

2.

White air
altogether white
above a plaza so immense
it even swallows up its very city,
as large as country, large as nation,
where East came to its furthest West.
For many thousand years
sky also violent
behind white air. And so:
the air now only slightly blue
against which birds
colorful doubtless at creation
now black against white air, seeming
as heavy as exhausted hearts.
And yet no, no,—no weight at all
against white air, the white,
the white, white air,
the only slightly blue white air.

3.

A memory in time. Such
pictures of a path not to be taken!
How to detect at core of heartbreak
the reason for it. To glimpse a youth:
senses were sharpest. The youth far gone
into another country. Another suffers daily
one entire life the change had to be made
in circumstances. These same set life on fire
and burned it to a scar on a single page.

Blind for so long now, deaf too,
no pleasant odor ever touches nostrils.
All senses dormant, paralyzed,
joy subject to an endless absence.
Now passage from the guilty
to all *his* others: these animals walking
around, wounding, killing, all other
animals in orgies of extinction,
looked at as *animal* and not as "animals,"
bring tears to the soul's eyes. Rise
to the face. Down each side of the nose
warm liquid pearls. Hatred & love
drinking each other. Liquid streams
below the stairs. Marriage should
never be allowed to perish:
cause, circumstance, life whatsoever.

4.

The going up, the going down
of fortune's wheel,
broken, defeated feet, his own,
clamped onto that same wheel, trying
to keep afloat. A cane helps manage.
She in the thighs of fortune
now taken in, now harried out,
trapped in the stench of everlasting change,
the highs & lows, failure called "life"—
as if this dread concatenation
of our haphazardries
could bear the name of "life..."

5.

Dream invocation:
Do not close this marriage,
nor even try to close it.

True marriage does not die
entombed among the stairs
though it may sleep forever.
Standing above its time,
swallowing all
like a black hole at heart
of this gigantic galaxy,
eats all, drinks all,
of the persisting life,
drinks human blood:
the blood reddens the skies
sunset & dawn.
Follows the anticline.

6.

Beautiful child of the deep stars,
svelte loveliness in bridal night,
food of profoundest scholarship,
parsing the future of this eon:
hover above collapsing stairs
to sing our coming epic. It will
not die. It will not die. And yet,
a hundred years from now Fez
will have gone to seed, to blindness,
melted to desert, unrecognizable—
if not into a mess of skyscrapers
born from the avarice of mindless men.
Opposing infidels will swarm into the sets
of this film unrecorded, into this movie
of our crippled days. Legs cramp at night.
The stairs have not yet fallen. To know
of death, yet not believe in it, this is
the rich commodity men know as hope.

7.

Behind the biblical, much further down,
below Fallujah, below Ramadi, below
Sumer, lower, behind the ground-down
bones of our originals, the first-born pain
of walking up & walking down twin streets
off which all beings, blinded, deafened, broken,
sell out their gross existence to an only bidder.
The you, the you *has* seen the eyes of this,
and heart, and felt the central core of this:
the you calls for upending
of all this poverty—while the rich flow,
terrace to terrace drinking the mint of heaven.
Now that you've left for foreign parts,
try climbing in your sleep,
continue climbing and inhabit us
trying to reach the terraces. The sky revolves
into our revolution, each part apart.
The muscles of our legs unwinding down
to pain, the nightly pain, dreaded paralysis.
The terraces because, from them, only from them,
the visage of the holy city—foundation
primal, most imperial—the city
of a prophet and his laws and, beyond laws,
an ocean of light in the brazen sky. The terraces
now reached at last as the sun sinks. From which we
recognize oceans of light in our own mastery.
The stairs now climbed. Not to be climbed again.

Fez, Morocco, 2014

THREE: IL PICCOLO PARADISO

Wohin wir uns wenden im Gewitter der Rosen,
ist die Nacht von Dornen er hellt, un der Donner
des Laubs, das so leise war in den Büschen
folgt uns auf dem Fuß.

Wherever we turn in the storm of roses,
thorns light up the night. And the thunder
of the leaves, once so tranquil on the bushes,
tags in the wake of our heels.

—Ingeborg Bachmann,
tr. by Nathaniel Tarn

IL PICCOLO

You have made here,
                 she witnessed,
      looking at
the assemblages, a small,
a piccolo,
      a paradise,
for us to bask in and,

                at this time,
in this here world, right now,
with no beatitude of any kind,
but just these latitudes allowed:
               hope or despair
and not a jot of will to help
      make sense of it.

The reading mind,
flowing among its flowers
for these—make no mistake—
are volumes of the inner heed
      and not of botany

wallows in satisfaction, a small but
genuine satisfaction
to sink in, or remain
         at strict attention

where all things you could name
as pleasure, joy, or... ecstasy
have faded ineluctably while
      self, in pain, condemned

to life without parole
            (the inner/outer wars)
looks out the window of our time
failing to notice, passing by,
                that life you failed to lead
when there was time and reason to construct it.

IN A STATE

One ("I," "You,")
      always present—
not having had

      a single moment
even of best
      at any time in world
(needs stressing: "best")
      without the tooth
(needs stressing: "always")
      of anguish at the neck—

and everyone on earth
           including dead ones still awake
      closed in some state

keeps them incarcerated,
         cooped in a single word,
repeated "going forward,"

so that:
a call goes out from state to state
      trying to break the glass

stronger than any steel however
they use to build the great machines
states can be locked in for the sake of silence

      weaving from place to place
      and time to time
      until no time is left

for any call, for any mailing
to any office, posing as state,
      calling as such,

unrecognized behind its flags
"I," "You," did not design
not knowing codes or kingdoms' keys.

READING THROUGH SLEEP

Reading re Revolution
in an ancient realm,
recalling recent ones
            even among the flowers,
right here,
under our noses—
                and yet no blood
runs from our noses
            to pool with theirs—

negating the terror,
                dissolving it,
                unable to dream it home,
to make the nightmare signify
                inside this climate,

falling asleep
                in sheer exhaustion—
            not through exhaustion
                as normally experienced
                        but by
collapse
                of the imagination,
                    of our desire—

a lashing, lacerating wind,
moves Paradiso's breath along with it,
leaves earth unable to inhale

for we are dead asleep
            who have in no way died
but by the death of others

and even this untrue
            all elegy abolished
            and overridden
for the whole history of these
            our disciplines
              "going on future now,"
         they need to keep on claiming—
        unknowing wherewith "go."

MOMENT

Who have never died
have never lived
A moment at the heart

parent to all of time
        wakes at a certain hour,
a certain second

could not have been predicted
        by "all the wise of China,"
wise of whole universe.

Wake! Wake!
for love of all you've ever been.
        Remember to remember
there is no other space,
no other time you could enjoy
        or truly live—as if a flower,
let's say my great white spire

unearthly high (tall as yourself,
        tall man, sharp tempest)
of white Delphinium,
        had stood beyond all reason,
had not been broken down
        by winds of such violence

as no year in this place had blown
with such fury, such indignation
that you'd forgotten how to still

                the suffocating mind

and now recalled seasons inhibited
by far too little patience
            for anything to matter

more than twin stars recalling you to life
        the sister brides
like *two* white flowers this round
        among n-thousand more
            inside that burdened heart,

holding the body to its daily day.

A SPIDER'S PRISONER

Far from this house
empty of visitors:
        no roads,
        rivers, canals
in the surrounding mountains
        to bring them in,

an empire surfaces
        through mist and cloud
        invisible at first—
valance-buried spider
        becoming fat on tribute—
            from his spiderlings.

Each year
manifests news
from very distant places
of imperial triumphs
and the establishment of spiderlings
            on available thrones.

        Their webs now cover planets.
They even reach into this place,
        gardens around this house,

We swallow bile and poison
bowing at undiluted shadows,
        indebted since childhood.

Throughout our time
the house's memory has faded—
behind the curtain:
that primal spider window.
        Why do you write of it

even now forgotten
way back at birth.
How do you manage to
                    remember?

VEIL

Behind this,
way, way, away behind
this, we may guess,
it's termed...
this veil
this all-enveloping
        gray veil
fusing all life to ash

(even the
"rose:"
mother infinity,
angel of color
circling infinity),

worn night and day
        of every day
of every holy year
        and each unholy—
what is the difference!

Behind this
way way way behind this
    veil
        adhering to the skin
since birth,
erasing a whole life
        night after night—
no remedy to pull you through
        but endless work—
the whole darned voyage

What is this thing,
unknown, hence unrecorded,
completely lost to any sight of ours
        anything known as sight

even in Paradiso—
    (you call *this* Paradiso?)

if not some thing we've heard
        evoked
but never understood,
        thing "happiness"?

THE PRICE

The thought of beautiful women
        opens the eyes of mind,
burns to the bone as well.

Bone: they too will earn
        in the last accounting,
        get thee... a nunnery,
        bone turned to ash in fire,
red shift moves out forever.

A single fraction of this universe
now visible—dark matter and
dark energy—dissolves the beautiful.
        Black holes swallow.

Then there is the thought
of those who are not "beautiful"—
women and men
who run the mortal risk
        of never opening a life.

But who can measure
        who is and who is not
in any eye believed accountable?

Leading, again,
to the innumerable lives,
open or closed, each lived itself
        alone, trapped, doomed,
never to be another than themselves.

This will break breakage. The
        galaxy explodes; the fate
of any joy there may have been
        in gambling on humanity

        fades incommensurably—
cannot be bought or sold,
not even told, not paraphrased,
                not even parsed.

ANGELS

Trained from the get go
for flight against all gravity—
        bars, mats and wooden horses
under their feet and hands—while mathematics
        default to access flying,

their whole existences
        like those of vestals
unable to enjoy anything else
outside the years of training, the
        cruel, barbed, the unrelenting, training:

all smiles when winning,
        and idolized by the accountants,
tears streaming when they lose
        left out to weep in the arena's
traps, without a thought

for their short shelf-life else,
           life of caged birds
feathered before their time—
        the daintiness of debutantes.
Then—flowered and bemedalled,

numbed in those interviews with the accountants,
bathed in the blather of triumphalism,
        rehearsing the same batch of words,
over and over like machines
what!—some two hundred words! no more!

the high-pitched soul-less voices,
the same dead vocab the culture mumbles
all the way up to Power and beyond:
its dumbed-down populace all ears—
        (Bumper sticker:
One Nation ... Under-Educated)

while other nations wonder at
        which mindless generations
they will be led, exterminated, by.

THING

Passing from time to time—
so if you think the pass is timeless,
you have
          one more think coming:
for pass, known as "eternity,"
          the dead call time.

It is not possible
to hold in head, to
get one's head around
          the notion of
                    a timelessness, even as

it is not possible
to totally ingest the thing called nothing,
to totally imagine lack of thing,
                    of anything
you could call *thing*

so as to have in mind
a hold, a touch, or a caress,
or pure punch in the throat
          "of your worst enemy"
and then behavior.

Even by the attempt to stress
to overcome unthinkables by stressing
          as in, say,
"nothingness of nothing,"
          still you will not defeat

how long a life will take to live,
on the only hand.
          How endlessly thing death is.

MAYA

Figure her turn of neck
bringing the head round,
        fixing the eye's position,
as it looks down on the embryo,
or small child alongside.

Her hand now reaching down
as if from sky to earth,
        the badge of ownership,
label of one lifelong possession
linking the two divisions,
(as by crab pincers),

of all our knowables. He,
meantime draws an imprint:
        birds' feet on sand
message transcribed in letters now,
burnt into memory. They meet

where the nature of stars,
fierce fire of stars,
flames time into earth's surface,
recites the chemists' formulae
        for all of movement

as if they knew (intimately)
the child's decision as it walks
nobly, nobly it must be sworn,
into the future,
where, in another text,

it would be walking into
        a solitude enduring
into the fading of all worlds,
        the end of history.

Therefore the flower.
Therefore the bird.
The universe.
Therefore the crab's
persistent pincers.
Therefore the void.
    The moment.

BOOKS FALLING

From the ultimate skies
books made of light
       fall toward earth
asteroids in suspension

taking incalculable years
to reach their breath—
from which they waltz
          interchanging colors
at every cloud

into the throats of angels
knowledgeable seraphs
             singing a
music heretofore unknown

life lived in secret thus
until receivers wake
among the earthly landscapes,
gather the books as visions.

Receivers still as mice
       at their own altars
put life in balance
       reciting the books
as if they were to lift them,
       they the receivers,
into the living skies

and clothed in feathers
from immortal birds,
       these same receivers
       now fly to friends on high,
begin to sing their recitations—
no further help from books.

ANOMIA

The only answer
to all this madness
      (*you* know *which* madness)
      is surely to lose
the order of the mind.

The fall has been occurring
it seems from the start of time—
while there was one break
         at that very start
involving single skull

      ensuring language.
And loss began:
word after word
     precision strained for,

then, when not reached, name,
name, a dozen names,
     name after name
until the conversation,

     like a field
parched by the rarest drought...
and the mind itself
     could not ensure

an order more, any distinction
between its sound and none.
     Only the trees
offered suggestions:

that whole vast cape of verdure
     chevelure of earth,
the very icon of inheritance,
     a silent concert very loud—

but plants not trusted
       to know the truth
with no one ever sure
       of his or her name's nature
of its exact, its proven definition.

SLEEPER

Now, she is quiet now,
inordinately quiet,
sleeping in fact—
        sleep of the just—
among the longest shadows of the land.

The language sleeps
she is not there to speak it,
it is forgetting
        word after word,
soon there will be no tally
        to say the possible,

to sing the wakening
which needs its music.
        Behind the lids seemingly closed
the open glare
        of human heaven
stares on continuous,
waiting for the conception,
the embryonic start-up—
        its light already reaching
for flags and banners,

black weapons, propaganda,
gold acid, cloth for burials,
        green monuments,
food for the saved
        (burned or alive),
the haunted faces of some children
        rather than others.

ARRIVAL

It is the casualness of death
entering now, yesterday, tomorrow
            so unimportant,
so without airs and graces—

            surprise
that it could happen small now
            and any time close by
instead of some big happening
            shifting whole life to grief.

"Who have never died
have never lived:"
            a moment in the heart
parent to all of time—
waking one dawn, unshaven,
so undetermined in the maze of days.

What's wrong with the word "dying"?
That all the noodles have to "pass away":
my wife "passed" yesterday, my husband...
            maybe he "pass" tomorrow:
            imbecile fate of our whole language.
Illiterates "passing" us all.

Or "Mother Nature."
What's wrong with plain old "Nature"?
Who in their hell of hearts
            without more euphemism
ignores nature as Mother?

As close to you
            as the wrist watch
on your own wrist:

time tells the twisted story
        of a departure for no arrival,
a song for no one singing.

HEART. MODE RECALL

Sign: Cancer

Heart. At the everyday,
at every hour, at every moment,
            shattering out
      of branches:

lobotomized and shell-shocked hawk
            in every which direction
knocking its head on walls,
mirrors, ideas of every kind,
and cannot fix on any vein of prey.

Called down, hushed, pacified,
from sky to sea—
            from sea metamorphosed:
crab-shaped,
            enabled now
to hold each universe,
in its perfected pincers—

heart peaceful rests,
            in very center.
Every and any thought come up
are calmed to wakefulness.
Everything else at the circumference:

that other ghost
all reason day and night,
incapable of any show of heart
            afraid, deathly afraid
to acknowledge love—
so left *you* in a heart attack,
            sin of tautology:
(mute, amicable friendship).

Circumference you said moments ago:
there, there, in perfect circle
round the unmoving silence,
a motionless, immobile, back to roost,
this heart of all the hearts impossible
            never to perish.

Your Paradiso, born to annihilate
immense outlook of hatred,
itself now wakening:
(endless acres of snow),
            now breathing easy
            until the only miracle
this earth has knowledge of—
the single ivory shoot
rises once more. All smile and domicile.

DEFINITION

What you are put into
       without permission asked,
and taken out of
       without permission asked

What is never explained
       neither for a before
nor, more importantly, an after—
so that the purpose of it
       never revealed
haunts the whole pass called "time"

in this you are supposed
to find the thing called "joy,"
to thank whatever maker
       you can serve up
          to your imagination,

to change all visibles,
make beautiful a manifest corruption,
hear, speak, sing, paint
beauty
       into every equation,
to elevate your taste,
update the swallowing
       into a Paradiso

Flag of the nameless.
For three, death is impossible:
witness the music.
For two, *idem:*
witness the music,
For one, possessor of a name,
       it can be done.

2012–14

FOUR: FIGHTER PILOTS

(EURYDICE, SR. LT., RISING
IN RE & TO: ORPHEUS, CAPT., SETTING)

In memoriam Lydia Litvyak,
Heroine of the Soviet Union

ONE

One day these talks with my dead husband will be written down and published. I walk and talk with him every day she can.

Ghost in these forests near the battlefield. I imagine he is coming to fetch her. But he is the live one in the mind.

Perhaps I did not know I loved him until the day he died.

Pilot poet: not many of those. Sky mourning over Stalingrad.

I find it impossible to believe in those who write *"off writing"* and not off—what? What should they write off?

The red-rose-cities-half-as-old-as-time are being written off all over many planets

and I can't see anyone rebuilding them. Or even planning to.

Someone has notified me that he is living half my life. I would be easier to persuade were he a she.

Or, by immaculate conception, an it.

What are earth's possibilities when hope has melted like a cheap date? Losha dead in a stupid accident.

Or cheap ice cream cone on said date?

Something you wouldn't normally eat this side of Hades.

Now I sit in this forest, reading texts on Practice over and over: but to what benefit?

I keep the flies off my crotch lest my hand wander there.

Every now and again allowed such a walk. Which comes in devilish handy.

Perhaps, tomorrow, I can hike a while. In Siberia's direction.

Cosmology. Walking is difficult now with a broken wing. It trails behind me impeding progress.

Did she survive some say? prisoner? exile? mother?

I think not.

TWO

In her days as a racing pilot, she invariably believed she would kill myself whenever I read a story of a fatal crash.

More than any I know it made her height-sick.

The inconsequential nature of his consequence was that he won every race in which he and I competed.

How can so great a conqueror have reckoned without the Russian winter? (How can two?)

First solo memento on shirt-back showed my runway's number and the plane's.

Racing is an unforgiving sport, turning a glorified lawnmower into a killer within seconds of an incipient misjudgment.

There was the heaviest willow-snow out of Novgorod that year.

When he said her breasts were golden cupolas against the blue.

Writing is in a state of conquest. There is no defeating writing. The problem is its death.

A poet never gives up on poetry.

It has taken over all of communication theory and practice. Numeracy is no longer at stake.

The mark of a true poet is that she is invariably killed by his enemies—

Some three kilometers from Dmitryevka.

And that in every known case those enemies are my true friends.

THREE

She was not flamed at Auschwitz, nor downed in Bosnia, Syria, Cambodia, Tibet, Iraq, or Afghanistan—

yet lives in *inferno* all the days of his life and wonders how to continue walking.

It is because of a nameless cruelty whose face I know but hardly dare reveal:

because life would become impossible (technically) if she did reveal it?

Men come with music in their mouths... and poison in their coming. I used to watch it spurt from time to time when I held them tight.

To her breasts they loved it.

This is where Losha crashed while teaching his student tight turns.

Her husband cannot fetch her again, I must stay down. He is singing to the animals and the animals lie quiet.

These very large leaves on which all is written—save her particular pain.

This ocean of pain that has lost its scripture.

So many years ago he left and only yesterday. Forgiving he goes, begging forgiveness.

They will miss her, Y'all. In the end, miss me.

Snowing above the Soviet in a far distance. Irkutsk? Kursk? bygone Borodino?

Ask how they ever possibly could have left me out.

Grease it in.

FOUR

It is a condition of our attachment to this earth that we suffer small matters acutely which—

cows lick their battle wounds in the field nearby and bellow out the eon—

seen from a star's perspective, or cosmic time's, are beyond absurdity.

Cows weep scalding tears for misbegotten children.

But how else could we be bound to this life? Or take it with any degree of seriousness?

Novgorod: peeing in a whirl of willow-snow and huge mosquitoes. Poor tail-piece!

For if once we were ever truly to see with a star's eyes, perhaps a million stars' eyes fixed on us as well, we could never breathe a single breath again.

I admired every one of her manifold cathedrals.

At the top of each steeple, doves open their beaks to sing. Did you say "sing"?

Rapt as we would be in another time, another space—and unable to continue this ridiculous existence.

Nearby too, stallions are dancing gracefully, reluctantly, waiting to leave for Petersburg:

it is because we are always leaving that I am here at all.

The Siberian Express is alongside ready to fly. From Leningrad they call it now.

Sit quiet for a little while before departure: a healthy custom.

Without departure, there would be no stay.

FIVE

Hand over cockpit door, just below shield, bracing herself.

Chest heavy with medals, 'chute harness clumsy over dress uniform: clearly a propaganda picture,

sees move toward herself, looking at it as if for talking (face to face), an image of woman looking very much like herself,

as if angels had been picked up in deep sky and ordered back down with the squadron.

All books on the heavy shelf fall down on top of me—shelf too: a woman killed by knowledge.

What is this to him if she is the presence within those letters, within the message of that intelligence?

His smile beatific, looking up, ideal-typical hero—as if smiling at the remaining angels.

And she the grace of all configured things, in perfect landing patterns.

That red star on her fuselage: heavily painted, outlined—as if contained thereby—in ivory,

not unrelated to the golden star she'll wear in future as decoration over the rim of her breasts...

And that Nazi *Niemyets* ace I downed who kept on saying

"But it is not possible! Dear Madam, just think of it: a woman!..."

That we speak face to face is miracle enough, being nothing more than one completeness.

Which they ignore completely between Atlantic and Pacific:

Lord, how dead among the stars the story of our young Republic

(which Russian Fall turns absolute to Winter)

when she was full of courage and a sweet daredevil among the fearful nations!

SIX

The killing continues in Guatemala (where my young man once worked), Ukraine, Poland, Germany—

as it once continued in Guatemala, Cambodia, Burma (where my young man once worked), Biafra, Kurdistan—

74

as it still continues in Guatemala, Rwanda, Iran, Iraq, Afghanistan.

Serial names often misplaced down here. These dead forget. Many moons ago. Many floods and much-much blood ago.

Day by day as the earth turns and with exactly the same unavoidability. Same haze of ignorance inside which we consume our consumptions.

Lest we go into the hills to forget that the race was ever imagined. Or neglect to observe

the paramount leader set over us as a certifiable moron with considerable dyslexia.

Humanoids become stick-insects while their brothers rob, sell, and profit from the food sent by other humanoids to relieve the stick-insects.

The revolutionaries kill the dictators and then turn into dictators.

I shit blood in my dreams and my uniform turns from saffron to dark red.

Can one live completely without hope? Never that surge of excitement, momentary heating of the pulse as something is "looked forward to"?

As if it had to do with the one greatest possible excitement of all human excitements: falling in love?

As if we had eyes in front of our heads instead of at the back of them?

Guard your back!

Is it all blind momentum, equivalent in faith to absolute inertia?

At an angle of attack too critical to log, I once soared out of these golden mountains:

quicksilver bird built to prey on those who would prey on the holy people.

It was dangerous in his young travels: the car door could be opened at any moment—and you, shot.

I saw Ulanova dancing once, the *Assoluta,* on one of my furloughs.

She was as lovely as a bird flying,

Oh, my mother country!

SEVEN

That building stood in a small street in Smolensk, very close to this street's intersection with a major avenue—from which it could clearly be seen.

If Paris was the Capital of the XIXth century, which is the Capital of the XXth?

Conceivably the Third Rome?

In no way could it ever have been said that they had tried to hide it.

Men in black hats and thick side-whiskers cannot be missed in a crowd. Cattle wagons await them.

Because it was not her name, she hesitated every time it came up in conversation, almost exclaiming "that's me!"—and then holding her mouth abruptly.

Now, the two of them are standing on the rim of the circumambulatory path of the great golden stupa Shwedagon.

They are photographed, safe in their saffron robes—so very different and far removed from the ancient red.

Every time you see such a monument, I am supposed to think of the Founder's teachings.

It is my favorite color of dress when flying with him. Under the uniform.

But what you cannot help thinking of is the thousands of imprisoned rebels.

All is presence.

Behind that presence is an absence so old, I have forgotten its name.

It went Elo...., something like Ad...., never meant to be photographed, but certainly always recalled.

He had said something like: "In those days, her name was... And in this moment she is called (name) and tomorrow it shall be (name).

Which may concern me, or not, but reveals.

Long ago, before kinship ruled, I adored him.

EIGHT

From a distant desert at the center of the *mappa mundi*, a city calls relentlessly day and night to its inhabitants who no longer live there. The nuclear plant blew up and they left.

It is way past bedtime so that all species should be extinguished.

Even to that last mouse in our rain forests, that last ant eating its carcass.

So that you should finally return, should you so desire.

The invitations never got printed. His animals keep dying.

Like the great October call, now rescinded, it was addressed both to the people and to the peoples.

I spent decades wondering whether or not my father would call. Before he died. My mother before. My husband before. My children before.

Where the harps hung on trees, everyone waited.

It was felt that there should have been an invitation, some kind of indication that one was *wanted*, one's presence was required, personally,

that it was one, oneself, that they wished to see again.

And he would go back, expecting to see certain signs signifying that the right individual had in fact landed.

For of something should be born something—not nothing.

Or so it seemed to me, for a very long era: until I saw that nothing is also born of something—so that not even nothing is nothing.

How desolate the olive trees must be on those ancient hills!

This city, this forest, burning.

How empty the great white house in the city center!

A voice shouting: "Lion of God!"

The beast long since perished.

NINE

Out of the most beautiful childhood imaginable, I walked from the palaces of the kings into this existence:

immediate fame was mine the moment I appeared in the window, or doorway, or cockpit.

The syllables of that language run on the tongue like honey, soft as the whitest snow our willows weave.

There was no question of my even meeting myself on the path: she was immediately the self that all men recognized, marked out among all beings for love.

No one, in that time, ever loved another without some secret sorrow that he, or she, was not in love with *me*.

The city was so wide—tall buildings seemed very small by the side of its avenues.

It was endlessly cold there and the only blues were those of river and heaven with shards of gold from temple domes cutting into them both.

I linked all work with that epoch through my own work: it was as if I had come on earth to bless every conceivable kind of labor.

My profile rendered the time in hours, minutes, and seconds exactly.

In all memories, I shone from then on like a white rose; the rose that, among all roses, had given the gift of vision.

Some say, of my fuselage, not a rose painted there: a lily. Some say no flower.

Some say flowers in the cockpit trashed by male pilots. Unhappy that women flew. Legend.

Walking like that, among princes, popes, bishops, great commanders, decked out in plumes and feathers—but as a human and not a god. How did he do it?

The Emperor died. The whole lot shot.

TEN

It was I in a long black gown with a slash of sky-blue at the hem, the perfect replication of his anima.

Far off under the trees, her voice soared over a game:

a game as sophisticated as a divine child's, a little sharp.

Black quilt of cloud half the sky's size, rain fringe at either end.

He had felt many times the planet trying to fight him down like that erstwhile angel—and now: that it wanted to kill him.

The voices rising in chorus as if to bring all the planet's quarrels once and for all into one universe of discourse—

though every voice could also be heard of itself and reasonably happy.

A noise of delicate shifting as of cloth at the elbow of a sage when he has comforted you.

Oh that my heart knew music like hers and I could teach it to my fluttering mind to bring it into steady flight!

Overwhelmed—and drowned out entirely—by the luminosity.

And that I could finally land this aircraft on a manicured field.

Dead as well as alive he will never cease to be my husband. Losha!

None other than those skylight nights of Petersburg ever produced conversations as intense as this. And I never cease to be wife.

Which is how she flew, at the end, right into the mouth of her ultimatum. Three *Niemyets* fighters caught her among searchlights.

Like the birds at St. Lawrence Island, on the world's other side, going round and round like the ghosts of the other dead—

(those who had not been fetched and would stay below, those who had never flown)

as if they were exiting a western star and entering into an eastern one before returning to the first.

When her wing rode high, shadowing the blinding ice below.

Of wisdom which is the world to come and of flight—which is this world.

Making herself up by little increments.

For it follows that, if the attention be evenly divided, all things must return to having the same flavor.

Kentung/Rangoon/Mandalay, 1959—
Suzdal/St. Petersburg/Kiev/Novgorod, 1992—Santa Fe/Los Angeles, 2010

FIVE: EXITUS GENERIS HUMANI

*Angenommen kann wohl mit einiger Berechtigtheit
werden, daß sich das Nichts-als-lustig-und-munter-Sein
die Zivilisation zu beeinträchtigen eignet. Zieht uns das
Ausschließlichliebliche nicht hinunter?*

It can no doubt be asssumed with no small justification
that never being anything other than jolly and merry is well
suited to compromise civilization. Does not the endlessly
endearing drag us down?

—Robert Walser, Microscript Text 200,
tr. by Susan Bernofsky

EXITUS GENERIS HUMANI, I

I. VISITOR

i)
Today, in a passing moment at the rear garden,
sees, hidden back of *chamisa*, a golden seedling
of the dead, something he had not ever planted—
ambassador from light—a newborn sunflower.
Exhilaration. Long song rising spontaneous,
a song from opera rarely performed, unknown,
he owes to Pyotr Ilyich and would embrace him
for it were he alive. (Somehow had been most
moved by those his sufferings Pyotr could never
share. For songs of love, for melody, this man
had few or no competitors.) Major discovery late
that same morning: no moment dedicated *in toto*
to *itself* could be other than *joyful.* Can recognize
joyful that have not spoken it for eight decades?
No "sitting": with sore back, desperate legs & arms,
interminable cramp & dormant buttocks (allegedly
existence-in-the-moment): you call *that* by the holy
name of *joy?* How *can* one live-in-moment when
it depends on previous moment and breathes into
the next? When care has terminated in the realm
of meaning (determination to do good to animals,
humans, cultures, societies); when it has fainted
in a sandpaper wind of wounded hope, depression,
(life as the preview of the realm of hell); when there
is nothing left to do can count achievement in its
repertoire; when all's absurd and thus acceptable—
then and then only, sing the melody by Gaia, by the
Illusion! Then and then only can moment and the *joy*
be imbricated on each other: for why condemn an off-
hand moment to misery? *Carpe* you imbecile! Why
not? What else can there possibly be to do and matter?

ii)

That you, who filled a life heavy as lead, mournful
with cries and curses, could suddenly love like a
lion this dying world, this *pourriture* of time, this
perishable race! And suddenly be seen to smile
when asked how the hot time of day would sit with
you, be heard to answer, it is fine, *f, i, n, e,*—as if
meaning held in such terms your state of mind, this
was akin to "miracle." Brought by the sunflower.
Next a.m.: sun's a stalk three inches off the ground.
Flower & leaves all gone. Her light is smothered. A
traveling rabbit ate the show and left no calling card.
Foreword to the whole garden perishing of drought.

Imagine a person who lays on other persons
cri/mi/nal/ly and with rash gain of wealth,
a problematic in which they will be trapped
for the remainder of their lives and which,
short of the arts of geekdom, they will not,
in a zillion years, be capable of solving.
Means that, for all those countless eons, the
system will engender problem after problem
which men will waste so many hours of blood
& life resolving, assuming they can be resolved,
not to bring into mention, or to amendment,
the most excruciating anguish ever suffered,
amounting often to blind and unadulterated rage.
As passion for "security" continues to melt down
every aspect of culture, of human intercourse—
all human persons legally become an endless
list of names, i.d.s and passwords—which they
will find impossible to pin into their memories.
All this goes by the terms "extreme frustration"
and "learned helplessness." At the sad end, any
advantages the system may exhibit are lost in the
disaster of the mind. All revolutions kill at the least
one generation. *La conputa* is sure out to kill *me*.
Imagine now grabbing a single *techne* criminal
(for there are many) and keeping him at mercy. Let
us say "him" it is the simplest, no way prodigal "her."
Mind plans, to show your *bona fides,* to prove that you
are *very-very* and quite close to madness, a form of
misery felicitous. Take first the criminal and free his
testicles from their worn sack. Assemble the vast sums
of money, stocks and bonds, the criminal has gotten.
Open the body, skull to toe, causing as much by way
of pain as possible—all this without determining said
body. Record whatever screams the criminal may utter.
Stuff into cavities "family treasures," *gelt*, shares, and
documents. Skin the abomination and trash remainders.
Then archeologize a burial mound in the archaic fashion.

Cause death-gods' hairy scalps to show above the sand
at the pit's floor. Lay burning coals into the pit and lie
the living body on them, then cover up the mess with
shit & sand. You have now dealt with one honored and
honorable to his society & yours, gladdened by women,
most prodigal in gifts & fat exchanges; one decorated
by many kings & presidents, granted abundant riches &
rewards. At least, Villon rode high on sky. Read R.I.P.

3. VITAL SIGNS (THE POLTERGEIST)

i)

Take from the night. Walk in young light
with birds exploding at the heat. No one
around. How could there be: you have no
relatives close by—those at the very ends
of earth living the lives you cannot feel
within your bones? You *think* those lives,
you think repeatedly: find the connection!
There has been an ablation of all "family."
What is this: to be prisoned, locked inside
one life and never to get out, no matter what
the inside quantity "compassion"? They take
your vital signs before announcing "you die
of 'this or 'that.'" Medical Genius One says
"this," Medical Genius Two says "that." And
death has all dominion, never dies. A figure
sways and comes toward you with little steps,
the steps get smaller all the while and they will
disappear completely at last breath. She takes
you in her arms. The times have died before
you—"waiting for Godot." Or was it god they
meant? (Critics have sworn it.) Or Ludwig
Wittgenstein? Or how about Duchamp? Mini-
malists evolve your shroud, breathe on the
fire cremates you. Those other lives you can't
experience make themselves manifest. Collect
the knickknacks, take them away to fill some
other house with snacks. Can call those *stuff*.
And you need far more time to throw stuff out
or to dispose of it than it took life to die-for and
to accumulate. A loss of value fast overrides &
you & yours. No one accepts donated life no more.

ii)

The sun bursts out beyond these hills, those trees
begin to burn, you sweat your body out reaching

the top incline. With heaving breath, you wait a
little, before descending to the house. Rip off the
clothes, the socks, the shoes. Your poltergeist
hides single sock and you're left with the other.
You waste unnumbered hours searching for sock.
Whole house departs. A whole house disappearing
day by day—because the poltergeist. So there you
go, there have you gone! Smoke rises highest yet
above those loving hills at life's fondest farewells.

4. BURIAL MOUND NORTH

i)
Dream. Was it a dream? How can you tell
when the whole night has been a semblance
of awake, the first three morning hours as
well. A tender odor—as if some female soul
had been nearby. *Odor di femina.* Must have
been dream: no one's nearby. Da Mooze?
Too much perfume n' sex for *that* in this
befuddled air. Your fingers ache to follow
and pursue—grasp only air. The Aphrodite
recipe: definitely dream. This is the very last
striptease you may be doing. Tired of you
naked to no purpose and with no returns. On
the other hand, bent on *ad hominem* foul play,
Volva high up in her domain at the north pole
(we're talking ancient Norse) so many years
ago, nauseous slunt, with nothing but a kaka-
demic chair between her legs, disliked your
boldness in these matters, said so as she had
done before when dealing with contemporary
stuff—and she had wrecked careers. Those
northern priestesses and shamanesses, ladies
of death & desolation, war, poverty! Knew
nothing of post-skaldic poesy but gripped her
chair nevertheless—to fart when dealing with
postmoderns. Time to die, O time to perish!
All the foul pain will take departure over to
"eternal rest." There'll be re-entry by and by. A
leading, kakademic critic, phoenix-like, reborn.

ii)
The Mothers in the burial mound. Back into
them through all yr. offices, yr. studios, yr.
encyclopedias of collegial knowledge—the
only manageable entrances. What else is love
but re-absorption to the primal sea below the

mound? The earth, they say, is but a floating island topped by a single-sided *Sumeru*, model of every mound. The dream hangs in here during your whole walk round the block. Resting from its exertions. The exaltation lasted very little: despair (for the collective) has fallen back into depression (far too personal). How short the holiday! Yet birds keep singing in the same old trees. A path remains throughout the earthquake.

5. *DIVAS*

i)
Sky sapphires out such moments in the year.
One sings. Callas, Fleming, Netrebko, Georghiu,
whichever of the *divas* (our gorgeous slender
divas, no longer those fat ladies of the jokes).
Breaking the spines of demons, lifting the heart
and hot emotions ("such song's for the emotions"
said one shrink), making life tolerable for a brief
breath. How do I catch in words the utter reach
of distance, all distance stressed, the elevation
of a moment like a host—in which all possibility
is possible, in which every extreme that can be
intellected reaches its boundary, breaks skull at
wall, does not transgress its boundary, survives?
Where have our friends gone that I so loved
brooking all misery in fellow-feeling? I think,
I think the wind has taken them. Alone, oblivion
waits. How speak of it? How sing of it that am not
singing? How to record it in a book of "*angels*"—
supposing "angels" possible within a discourse—
for voice alone brings out their feasibility? Way
out beyond the flower, beyond the bird, such voices
to maintain this creature in existence. And even love,
the immemorial, buried so deep in universal mire,
freshened, talking again, speaking and even singing.

ii)
What do you know of *this*, poor dime-and-nickel
idiots, your heads buried inside your spines, your
asses plastered on your torsos, with all your "po-
etry" so called, your holy "writing," yr. broken lines,
yr. tortured speculations, yr. miserable disjunctions,
yr. footling, inexistent propositions: cough, tea, me?
Branded onto your teachers' single style—your only
hope of board and meals the selfsame prostitution,
drowning the truly-married out in your mediocrity,

can you not see a proposition perishing, philosophy
hauled bodily out of its pastures, shattered? Critique
never acceptable to flaming egos without the love
of art to balance out the hurt? Home, y'all, Home, out!

iii)
To "friends" no longer capable of love for us, that
wind took out into the depths of winter; and snow
(the angels' diarrhea, even the gods', what else?)
muting all other matter to itself, all other seasons
into winter, metamorphosed in a white storm to that
last level of the ice where the lost maws would howl!
Howling a silence *divas* alone may break when they
raise mornings to the sphere of fire! You've heard of
empyrean have you not? You burying the world in silt,
in sand, in silence, way back to the Triassic? "Want
to save planets? Kill yo'self." You are outdated, obso-
lete, forgotten. Our gods a' shivering. Do melt! Melt on!

i)
Vast lung of the vast earth: right lung now
floating. All the indigenous animalcules rising
and falling in the wrathful soup—since on this
lung and its green brachiates depends duration
for their genes. A viscous mass rises from *de
profundis*, wafted into the mouths of waiting
men (slaves of the floating). No longer food-
consumers. Oil-eaters: the excrement of hell
they swallow, to then regurgitate for a depen-
dent "loved-one." Deep forests: indigenous
resistance sets barbs will peel criminal snakes
back from their spines, scorch them alive. The
cruelty of rise and shine! Thus right lung sinks
& rises in the selfsame moment, with us paying
the daily shifting taxes and powerlessly calling
for a halt. Resistance yelps a halt, flies flags
in ancient capitals to warn its chiefs the time
has come: thinking they've won a battle when
they've lost a war. Ah Ecuador! Peru! Immense
Brazil! While the immortal slick spreads further,
in the lung. Paradise birds fall headlong into it,
the bat, the viper fall headlong—even the greater
beasts: cats, mammoths, megatheriidae, massive
heliovores still lurking in the forest mind, slump
headlong to the slick. They have no other hatred
deep as this, as all encompassing, those poor, small
slaves accumulating wages in the slick, gathering
not enough, never the threshold of enough. So hate
a swine sliming its dividends in distant corporations.

ii)
Meantime, in the left lung, a small and noxious pit,
the price of ages rises to the surface, the bones of
astronomic eons of past lives float upward through
the slick, revealing structures of a forgotten world

lived long before the oil. Bird surfaces, with wings spread out, and bat, with wings spread out, delicately made of dust here, pasted onto the present so that the future minds their shapes and destinies. (You see, we can insert a line of "poetry.") Touchingly sweet dead universes of dry selves, with all their friends and allies, rise in a shower of scales must be humidified so that the fossils do not crumble. A spirit knowing nothing of the smell of meat rises to sing. The earth with its two wounded lungs can breathe again a while (not very long for this is finals)—but little *momentitos* so that we may remember how air used to perfume our wilderness of heart in love with sheer existence when it ran free in our free throats... and unpolluted.

7. MAMMOTH EXCRETIONS

i)
Back from the cosmo-litical to loco-litical at hand. Zowee!
The *"Rio Rancho"* scene in dear old paradise. No *Rio*. No
Rancho—nothing new yet in this "New" Mexico. Colossal
spread of township over desert, pure, unadulterated, un-
prepossessing desert. A mammoth, vast as the You-S-A,
roaming this land, shitting as need occurs... and habitat,
cardboard-compounded, falls where they will. Ugly and
convoluted, conforming to some "standard taste" no one
outside has ever heard of. No fences, hedges, shrubs,
to sign the properties. From space to space in this catas-
trophe, the urgent shopping malls with all the dreamboats
known to "ci/vi/li/zi-za/tion." Walmart, Best Buy, Big
Mac, or Burger King... all needs are met. But it's now firm
the water will be wanting. The sinking aquifers of nearby
cities will *not* rejuvenate within some sixty years. All the
more likely for the excretions to fall back into sand. Where
will the people go (just like the Anasazi): invade the Texas
or the Mexico? A no-gold Gold-Rush into the California?

ii)
Today an article on Izembek, a Refuge at the very tip of the
Alaskan thrust into the cross-to-Asia scene. Vast multitudes
of birds, innumerable birds, congregate here, Springing and
Falling, for the refueling will take them countless thousand
miles to their life destinations. The place a Park, inviolate in
theory. Now minute population on the Refuge edge calls for
a road right through the Izembek to reach a border town for
groceries and such. The population problem. End of the You-
S-A? The politics is shit. The economics shit. And the reli-
gion shit. Bright dreams once dreamed in that small hut on
Eastern shores one July Fourth now Mickey Mouse. But why
not cut the nation into seven parts: all such environs sound?
Persistence must persist undoubtedly. I'm of this nation for
good or worse, I'll live the rest of it. To die here is my hope.

iii)

In silent tropic forests the Rats have crept and get to work. A tree
comes down. Bribes to the ranger to desert his charge and take
substantial naps in hut. Bribes to the men who drag the logs down
to the river. Bribes to the watchers at river's edge hailing the rafts.
Bribes to the raft racers braving the rapids down to a silent pool.
Bribes to the canoe coxswains take logs from pool to roadside.
Bribes to the middlemen move logs from rafts to trucks. More
bribes at police check points on road to logger mogul's station.
Bribes from the logger mogul to the government. Bribes once
again to the export guys. Who bribe the buyers in distant lands.
Who bribe *our* buyers to source illegal lumber. In the vacant
forest, the land sports oil palm in its ugliness, its dust-dry mi-
litary ranks, its killing fields for infant animals lost there and
starving. Meanwhile the Rats eat monkey meat, bush soup with
menaced species drowned in it. Cash waltzes round the universe
filling our time, our jobs, our confidence. Whether the planet goes
to waste or not, what matters is our jobs. "Better to die tomorrow
than today" the proverb goes: these children who need feeding
must be fed, no matter they will go to war a little later for their
fathers' sins. The water wars. Crop wars. The population wars
& "*more*"! We have forgotten dearest goddess, we have forgotten!
Whatever our persuasion, we now *take*. Land *and*, sky *and*. *Grab*
air, water, forest, oil, our wholesome diamonds, rubies, emeralds,
and—leaving the first born natives of the earth homeless, dead.
Our forest fathers at their work dream their opium dream. Our
mother faints, losing her arms dropped one by one into the forest
rivers and floated down for sale. World sold to whoredom now!
Just never said enough. But word unheard, warnings silenced.

8. COLD UNMISTAKABLE

i)

Raising the images of birds up out of books
since they no longer fly the fields and forests,
no longer darken skies in their migrations, or
sing dawn out on greening boughs. Remembering
dawn walks, a land deserted—no other humans—
thinking the love borne for one bird atop her tree
outweighed the love for one last human race. Ice,
Ice. Ice now turns again. Not some sheets moving
down to cover some cold parts, but a totality of
ice, the world made ice down to its bones, and,
Look! there'll never be another broiling summer
to melt this ice away! Seasons disappeared. A
flatness about earth and sky; all lines run parallel,
not up and sideways, old authenticity. Change,
most "eternal" of our principles, motionless. Such
distant memories of deal termed "Climate change"!
Is it because, before the ice, a fire had blazed, razed
every landscape (nature or culture) down, propelled
to final, wandering loss the earth's last populations?
Today, far off beyond the nearest ridges, the sound
of one sea howling, one sea barking: all prey has
faded from the land; there is no food; even the taste
of food has been forgotten. The rabbit you remem-
ber suffers a new leukemia: loses its use of limbs,
spring of the muscle, fire of the blood, falls now
from left to right, from right to left, trying to eat
the bird seed scattered here. And is no food for us
who lie at home on beds of nettles, waiting for
the old lady in her wagon—she never seems now
to remember us. Her priests emasculated catamounts
wanting from us only a sandwich where there is no
sandwich: interminable begging. Ice given in return.

ii)

In the selfsameness of the latitude, it's all one taste
we fill the mouth with—whatever we may swallow,
stiff with brine, reaches no novel flavor in our throats
whose backs all parched, all burning, will fail to
recognize that *joy* once married in our hearts to each
beloved mouthful of a life. So that the lastness when
it comes one day out of earth's loss, the lady in her
wagon reaching out a pinkie—why merely backs us
where she'd engineered us: each single his, or hers,
into an origin no longer loved—and so much less
worth waiting for through our unending holocausts.

i)
With intent. Never explaining, never justifying,
never requesting anything for *self* (its vulpine
face, ferocious eyes), determined on a task no
one had trained her for, no one ever suggested
the task was feasible for one of such low caste.
Year upon year, into insanity, the move enacted
to breaking-point. Had not enrolled for such. Not
drafted. Trees laugh, sing, pray for this one while
this one prays for them. Sits among waves waiting
for the next mission. No one is ever at this concert,
no one ever configures music will continue. There
is no possibility that solitude resolves itself, that
conversation can turn thinkable, that there might
be some contact between the proposition and the
solution. Who can imagine a solitude so massive
the consciousness of other cannot be formulated,
spoken? But can be *shown*? A fright to neighbors
who may ignore her, but hear her sometimes being
her being. How beautiful the scene that this takes
place on, how lovely forth to tears the landscape
plays: green alleys lined with flowers lead to vast
meadows; these to green seas beyond the visibility
today when flight is limited. This girl has never seen
a sea. "Not to be purchased I" says girl. "Succored
& helped, yes, but never, never bought" she swears,
refusing every shadow of any hard salvation. As if
there could be some salvation—in any different life!

ii)
Voice of a mouse, a timid mouse—unfitted to the
vulpine mouth which would devour this voice if the
scenario allowed it. O sweet beloved of ancient days
(beyond a thousand wars, always the same, always
from one disaster to the next—the characters pay no
attention), lover resolved, but grown inoperative
beyond the confines of the body, that body grown

immense as *terra mater.* And had not single son, nor
single daughter to populate the nation. On knees, mixed
herbs, mixed drugs, balms, elixirs, mixed all the cures
would lubricate the eyes—as if her sockets illuminated
heaven. The stars! I now remember: she never did see
stars. She was so much the day's light was this maternal
Earth, no night could drown a Sun she would forgive
if only love could manifest at last and enter solitude, in
such a way that solitude perdured. But now forgiven
and annealed. At last a pregnancy self-generated by this
love. O Child of light come down to visit us! Child of a
captured fire silver & gold! Child, driven, innervated light!

EXITUS GENERIS HUMANI, II

A. AS IF PHILOSOPHY

An awakening. But that nothing can leave its boundary,
to stray outside of it. Unmake the new. Return to zero.
Do not pass go. The sense of swimming in an undefined
possibility's air. The other is an I. Now you will hear
a buzzing of the world above you—to sting you till you
fry. Ah poet! so totally subjected to your genius theory
or U die. *Ich kan nicht wissen was in ihm vorgeht.* Death
as the wrist watch, closest to you heart. As close as heart.
When will you wear this? When will you ever listen?
Except, of course, under supratern discourse. Think:
it is essential to keep in mind, always to keep in mind,
not for a moment failing, that interruption is permitted,
indeed will seek you homing and never fail to find you.
As though it flew over the world, hope is committed here,
and leaves it as it is. Observing it from far below in flight
such divine heels waft you to disappear into oblivion.
All heavenly activity is shut. But lack of scientific trust?
The camera you bracket now to every creature's back:
you'll witness eagle soar, a lion pounce, slither of lizzies.
But all you'll actually see's a head looks sideways, back.
Technology has failed among its great successes. Again.
The first creations of the gods perished as sinning apes,
unable to praise their Makers, their Lord Substantiators.
Again, they tried to build the future for a *human* world;
the gods tried to be gods, the demons demons, breaking
over & over. Of brittle mud. Of splitting wood. To name
the names, honor the kings. And finally of flesh they wept
the future failure. Nothing has praised the true visage of
Earth—nothing has risen to the godlike level. A race alas
lacks all humanity. To be destroyed. Here come the latter
days, O *Ragnarök* washed in the blood of dragons! Those
cretinized by the religions (mostly the Abrahamics) sing
psalms finding no one will wish to save them. The giant
surface of a sea, seen from below by sharks, is the huge

mouth of hell, not one bird born up onto blinding air. It's claimed at last and graven down in rock: (laugh loud) that poetry ought to be written faintly stoned, as if philosophy.

i)

Look at parts of the wave but (even if), there is thus
boundless movement from each part to each other,
the ocean, still, nevertheless extinguished. *Bardis-
mally*, a fearful prophet drops down into your life,
encounters image, not in a mirror, but in manure.
A terrifying battle for sense to make some sense.
Never will s/he exclaim at an encounter with (wave
follows wave) for there is no discovery, only the
one wave simultanymous with all the other waves:
and thus with the whole ocean. Far much too much
of ego-satisfaction. What one illusion, referencing
wave, wishes to offer, above all information, is an
absence of gender difference. Wave permits many
voicings from water textiles' loosest to the most
firm entanglements (sailing to far Sargassos!). Thus
patterns reach to parallel in all their scintillations.
Over such wholes, she who should never seem a
visibility *is* seen in all magnificence. Below: scales
on the wings of flying fish, the multituding crests
of the one wave in its innumerable changes. Wring-
ing the changes of the cell, the paradise, the sentence.
Go home and rest! There is no transmigration! All
things have to endure the sempiternity! Interminable is!
                                        Isness of is.

ii)

Text into text, thought into thought & text: exchanging
souls. So difficult to enter and evermore to exit. Aha!
Especially when you ignore the locus is you aim for.
Such finding of the inner life has become desperate:
everything sunk so deep and far there is no light, no
tunnel. Heart, from too great frequencies of melting
in its solitude, has turned to ocean without lands that
can contain it: it is impossible to find a bearing there
from which some comfort may derive. You've died,

perhaps, and do not know it. Crimes you've committed without an end in sight condemn you to the gallows a hundred times—if justice could divine your heart and thus condemn you. All of us naked under our clothes the doctor said—but not naked enough. There would be murder in the streets, intense revenge, a hell of pain and cruelty from everyone to everyone if truth were told. Meanwhile, heart, liver, lungs: these three a *warning*. We crawl on laboring lately—as if human beings.

Hootless in high water. Not giving one for. The urge
to tears rends the insides, a.k.a. guts, from pubic bone
to throat. Birth of our inner waters mysterious as that
of certain secret rivers in the most fragile continents.
Now, tears suppressed throughout the conversation.
Back then. Need to relive the past without a hooter
contribution. Since poets' hearts are a world's heart,
dixit Herr Heine, then they must surely tear to shreds
in a terrible time. And you should curse at what the
sandman says in his silliest, arbitrating hours? On
back. Scents are the flowers' feelings says the same.
As if the ocean were the soul itself he swears again.
And should you be depleted re belief in soul? Back
off. The worst is entering a lion's room and finding
it quite empty. Yet, moments later, a lion roar rends
the blue sky over the palace. Where is the lion now?
Asleep on roof? Curled up among the battlements,
and looking down at crows below? The crows, the
ravens of our choice memories? Who walked in fields
of flowers—abundant temples by classic architects
filling the fields while, summer-mad, the bees drove
knives into the flowers gathering their honey and "O"
the sun burning its way through brain and sinews, with
maddening hopes, broke open *all* of memory! Out of
it steps the girl as if she'd never left us for the darker
side—as if her love were ours alone "forever and a day."

EXITUS GENERIS HUMANI, III

I. PARIS OLD

Mind now roaming where body roamed ago
thru fields, woods, forests, hills... valleys
& caverns. Our holy planet Earth summons all
bodies to herself—a flesh of glorious, ethernal
summer light. *Humeur / Humour / Amour*—
its incarnating process was discovered here
in these three bodies signifying choice: in time
beyond remembrance under these golden skies
frequented one time by a divining prince. (I
should remember and I don't.) One spelled
incarnate Love by name—the others Wisdom &
Imperium, but all were love here indiscriminate,
trapped in this memory. What comfort Earth has
now all man is meltdown, the insane race dis-
solved, while Earth alone remains inviolate in
her fertility? How I would love to bring around
that triad body now from memory—and live
with them alone, roaming their fields, woods,
forests, hills, valleys & caverns as the mind now
roams. Hardly a day forgets to bring, crossing the
winds below these eyes, some form the mind could
perish for—could "die-for" as they say today—yet
cannot. This helpless mind devoid of hands, of
mouth to speak its love, incarcerated in a useless
prison—that less and less is guarding anything
beyond some photocopies of judgment long ago:
when war roared on the Earth burning lost lovely
flesh and terminating every chance that body ever
held of keeping down the mind it manifested like
a frozen flag now failing on winter's battlefields.
The line attempts survival, time and time too it fails.

II. THE HOMER

Black Widow clambers up this bucket against a
stream of wet insecticide, long black legs waving—
as if to gather prey. What manifest multiple eyes?
Poisoned mouse, bucketed to drown for faster death,
scrambles in vain against a fall of foaming water. In
a historic town, sunk in a foreign land, Beggar roused
from his lethargy by passage of a Homer, intensifies
his pleading to a rim of tears. The desperation: deep
eyes in jet-black circles; a "Help me!" "Help me!" almost
screams and scatters pigeons, scalding heart: for real?
for theater? No way of knowing. Open scar pulses, the
never-healed inside the Homer's heart, also yells "help
me!" to itself—as Homer and his Beggar flood one being.
And sun then rises above eternal winter (ice not abating)
warming our blood & spirits. Homer walks into it, his
armfuls stretching out toward it. Sun's ivory rays, as if
bright limbs of some promised salvation, honor, salute,
wrap him, forgive him it might be—if such conceptions,
floating above black skies, our boundless provinces,
still sign and certify acceptance: some vast imperial grief.

III. THE GUEST

In memoriam Ernst Bloch

i)
A new guest in the body, foreseen, yet unforeseen:
for the last lost control has to be unforeseen. Do I
equate somehow this novel visitation with the final
run, as *I* foresee it, of the collective? I do not think so.
Futures and Pasts cannot hold up examined by the
mind and, as for Present, that mighty Present all talk
about as the one only thing to do, or see, or think—no
I don't think so. The verbiage masters have talked of it
as the sole enemy of the destroyers, but they themselves
are this destruction too, a loss of language. In the interior
the forests fall and all things in those forests also fall,
a famed diversity gone in that fall, like languages. Just
now, just one ago, last speaker of that given language,
unknown, barely recorded, barely understood, fell into
silence and the whole span of human history for you
fell also. "Idiots, I die for you!" said a Resistance chief
to *Wehrmacht* soldiers about to shoot him. A Marxist.
Masters, I lack the calm to navigate the giant ocean of
your writings (masters!), the nerves to hack your noise,
you that fill *agorae* with noise as loud as thunderstorms
over civilizations. I have gone deaf. I am going blind. I
feel no part of any thing in all these limbs extending
like some eastern god's multiple arms into all space.
The guest takes time, his time, her time: what is his or
her gender anyway? Lies down in body, gently questions,
thus endlessly—never awaiting answers, but questions
on—until night falls over the failing forests and the host.

ii)

This book, divided, reassembles. A wave, broken by
islands, regroups and follows on. Inside such waves,
vast whales move forward on the deep to reassure
my ears. You have heard those songs. How I wish I
heard them! The exile deepens, away from records,
away from words, away from understandings. ("I've
never read this book." Open the book finding my notes
from many years ago.) A mind floats on this giant wave
and never homes, never can home. Since memory is
severed, quartered, hacked apart—like lab brains.
Dissolving is the law: all matter breaks on wave and,
feeding it, abandons us forever in traceless afterlives.
Stop for a breath one moment: where is my book?
My book where shall I find it? Shrink said, one time,
with ferocious glare: "You do not even *read* your books!
You fail to *recollect* your books! You have no sight of
what they *talk* about!" Most true—but I am going blind.
My books grow in a jungle like blind trees without me.

iii)

Time for departure is assembling: the caravans drive
off with planet's libraries of books. Leaving this garden
far behind in which all lands are just one land, all nations
just one nation, now borderless, now passportless, where
vegetation bears same fruit, and where all creatures
work one same purpose. The walls are locked up now:
there is no homing. We break toward a future none will
see. The guest falls into sleep among our thriving sinews.

We will not have no war! No! We hate war!—yet when
these men in scarlet, black, dark green, for the most part,
descend our little local stage, pretend it is the hollow
Boreraig—where for ten generations M.D.'s "Great Music,"
the now lamented, was learned and practiced, we fall fair
victims to illusion. Come the Argylls, and Sutherlands,
and Royal Scots, and King's Own Scottish Borderers, Black
Watch and Royal Highland Fusiliers (I'll give them six
on five for rhythm's sake) yet now all pressed into a single
wedge—the "Royal Regiment of Scotland." The Army small-
erized! The Empire drowned, an island smallerized that was
so small already! How hold "tradition" when thus pressed?

---

                *"No prospect of eternal
life; no fullness of existence; no love without betrayal;
no passion* sans *satiety."*

                Feathering drums as gentle as
Spring rain enamored of its flowers; the nearly angry
shriek of pipes, roosters after their hens; the swirling of
all cloth, from a cock feather tip to the sharp knife pleats
under, and, there, over a hill, the "cavalry arrives" as we
would call it here—god only knows we love these ancient
enemies of the republic in anglophiliac glee—standing,
ovating, smiling with the wide smile of pleasure music
alone can grant ears deafened by contemporary wars!
Over the hill, with antecedent whispers of "Great Music,"
they follow down (as if they did not have to curve on the
small stage and re-appear); the thin red line of triumph in
our memory waves forward to the ultimate conclusion of
this time:

"Look! is that only the setting sun again? Or
(is) *a piper coming from* (so very) *far away?"*

The man
wrote he had read me dead in an obituary back in the old
country. I told him no, I'm well away in these far deserts.

"the body itself as, by movement of its own tissues,
giving the data, of depth"

Bombarding depth through past and future—often mis-con-
joined—to rankest abolition of the *now*. The *now* become
invisible. That done therein: invisible. Unrecognized. Flutters
of little pasts and futures furtively recognized by contrast. Oh
those parts will burn! What do you know beyond the latest
bellowing you're pleased to call our time's great "music,"
the latest hip-sway, latest grimace, and finger-pointing at the
empty air: Homer? Virgil? Shakespeare shaking his spear from
the old country you deny knowing as what established you?
Death of this empire amply provided by universal ignorance.
Way back beyond desire to live, the windows of this submarine
are dark. The complex depths have blackened them completely.
Tissues are frozen by such depths: tissues to burn. Great forms
of deep: the mammoth octopus, the dinosauric whale, have lost
their power to move. Will burn. Only at farthest down, in ever
deeper trenches, sulphuric vents throw up diminutives with life
inscribed in them, to further history. Men of a brighter day—if
such there ever is—remember darkness for it will come again!

Kingfisher-bright, a love of blue & green conjoined brought all
of this to bear. How can one bear? Bare bone will tell for flesh
will not achieve a recognition, be sung into the grave. There was
Propertius, oh, dear Propertius, the man with the one song he
burnished all his life, claiming this song would save him from
oblivion. No fear! Don't count on it! Quintus Horatius Flaccus,
oh, dearest Horace:

non ego, nobelium scriptorum auditor, et ultor /
grammaticus ambire tribus et pulpita dignor?

Sumer undoubtedly held out the similar.

the greatest
present danger / the area of pseudo-sensibility / anything
goes or / all is *interesting Or / nothing is. Opinion / has*
replaced all such.

A love of deserts, icefields, oceans—where presents can be
recognized and futures plotted. A love of jungles:

the intermediary, the intervening thing, the interruptor, the
resistor. self.

Soul. Action. Home: These are identifiable among the foliage.
Kingfisher flash, zigzag along the creek, rampant with snakes
and caymans. This, and then Morpho butterfly: O great winged
god-dess—these last to furnish blue identity with bliss. A-men.

The Head of State sleeps, dreams, plots, prophecies
and lies. The sky above him/her bright with pure light.
Head of State's consort dreams, plots, prophecies
and lies. The sky above him/her bright with pure light.
Chief Minister sleeps, dreams, plots, prophecies and
lies. The sky above him/her bright with seraphim.
The other Ministers sleep, dream, plot, prophecy
and lie. The sky above them bright with blue angels.
The judges, generals, servants civil and military
sleep, dream, construct & deconstruct, plot, prophecy
and lie. The sky above them bright with its rainbows,
planets, moons, meteors, stars, satellites & storms.
Lightnings as well. Comets & asteroids as well.
Bankers and corporation CEOs so wholesome all,
sleep, dream, plot, prophecy, collect their bonuses
and lie. The sky above them bright with blue ptero-
dactyls. Media producers, talking heads, celebrities,
announcers sleep, dream, plot, prophecy and lie.
The sky above them bright with its commentaries.
The common citizen thinks he or she exempt,
safeguarded from this woe but sleeps, dreams, plots,
& prophecies & lies. The sky above said citizen bright
with promises. O crammed with futures, dividends &
prizes! All will then turn toward the Revolution, kill.

VII. INDIVIDUALITY, SOLITUDES

In memoriam Paul Mus, Buddhologist

i)
Our small, low, tidy bushlings of the desert: hardly
can they be called by name of "tree"—each one
lone individual, not merging in the mass, into the
indivisible. Used to such trees by now, used to
such trees, unable to enjoy tall trees for very long
in other climates. At the same time, a terror of *our*
trees, an overwhelming fear of their aloneness—or
rather of division: for self into a multitude cannot
be joined together in discourse or in thought. Fear
of a sole, an absolute desire a tree faces from seed
to drought (which brings it down so black) under
relentless desert suns! And such as well the sight in
any crowd, a dagger in the chest at such a thought as:
how is, say, just *one* being in this crowd able all
by itself from livid dawn to tarnished dusk, from birth
to death, tentacles out, tentacles in, now, now & then,
second by second, minute by minute, hour by hour,
and day by day, hundreds, thousands of days—how
can it be *itself* out there and nothing other in the dark,
that dark—whether of day or night—unending dark
night of the body philosophical? An unrelenting dark
of such a solitude as no known thing, human or animal,
kin or affine, parent, child, lover, friend can ever put an
end to? How this great crowd of solitudes speaks at
our solitude, or does not speak, most times unwilling or
unable so to speak, so that we perish at the very final?
In a distortion only grows, never diminishes and—
choking on thoughts of its own break—sneers even at
the vastness of the skies, interminable marching of the
galaxies, the furthest stars, most solitary stars, moving
along their paths and out beyond all knowledgeable end,
horizon to horizon, orb to orb, into a definition of infinity?

ii)

The solitudes are set to grow and to distend until they
eat, devour, digest all thought we know to be our own
(amended & expanded by the prophets we've matured
with). The empty brains of children rattle in their skulls
grown dry by much exposure to the sun. The sun, we
know, will harrow these poor minds until they prove in-
capable of any further good. *O mio ben*, the *agathos*, the
good: no serenade, no aria, no song can ever bring to life
again that imageful potential... The daffodil has rotted
in the earth, the earth dried in the pot, offered too long
to the relentless master planet. No matter how we move
against the stars, escape will be repulsed, frontiers will
never be erased, no ship will home in these demising seas.

VIII. RECENTLY ASSAYED

For Hölderlin

i)
On the left hand: chatter. On the right hand:
chatter. At center, the perfected stem. Ha! A
mind? society? (No: pseudo-Greek gymnasium
rancid with chatter.) How come the left, on
my own side, leaves me so still, so silenced;
the right catching at every word and a huge
wave, as if avernal, sweeps over all of mine—
tears rush to outsource rivers from my eyes
(tears yet! these adult tears!) since I will never
hear the end of it, never attain the goal of
peaceful, primal, unarchitectured gardens and
a perfected (*rose?*). A climbing, rising, flying
rose—to wreathe immortals. Attainment *never*
dreams of the attainment—attainment's moving
mountains, load of harassing effort: satisfying/
being satisfied, the one holding the other back,
the other holds the one, the joint outreach of
ecstasy's maternal cry never attained at once.

ii)
You ask me where I travel now. You assume
I know? (space). I travel to the islands of the
blest summoned by men one-time called *angels*,
(led by one model, the unhistorical, the mold)
where the heart's ship strives now to anchor,
after *les vagues inouies*. Finds harbor close
by sullen caves those once called *friends* haunt
in their sleep. No one on earth numbered therein.
Long tunnels in the caves lead to... "eternity."
Don't write. Do not attempt, in any form, commu-
nication. No calls, no telegrams, no e-mails, & no
texting to demand response: there's no one here
for you. (Here leave a space for new technologies
to come.) Only the hollow dream of our dead ocean

stretching around the world, its tribes of albatross
in non-stop fall around that world (but separated out
in solitudes can hardly be imagined by the likes
of us); the algae trapped round and around giant
Sargassos; the sharks extinguished, who'll never
eat your legs, caught in among them, (last few, last
few); together with all forests, drenching gray sweat
and perspiration, your own blood dying red the rain.

iii)
Illuminated heart, ancient of centuries, emitting
passion like the firefly—hot, destined, dedicated
as they say, to its own species: how did that hold you
through the domains of life, each realm of those a
different horror to be overcome by the unquenching
phosphorescence? You *rose*, boy in old man, stood,
with prerogative, launched the one likely compliment
which hit, or did not hit, the only target. As he stood
at a bridge one time, ancestor-like, master yet dumb-
struck, aghast at her disclosure to the light of day, the
lovelorn brightness escaping from her aura while lines
began to form—longer and longer ran toward a book,
with a collapse of stars to ground as yet another night
rose (yes, again) to sky. As a result of that: now, do not
write, do not communicate: there's no one here to hold
your voice, your hand as if they mattered—host gone
toward another place, his guests unwelcome, sight broken
down, day never now to shine again, nor even stars dead
high up there, nor any light whatever. You: silence now.

Trobardao Leu, & Clus & Ric

IX. THE LONGING & DESIRE FOR JUSTICE CONDIGN
TO THE END: A PRESEASON SALE

> I thought of the limitless vastness of the universe;
> I wept for the long affliction of man's life.
> Those that had gone before I should never see
> And those yet to come I should never know of.
> > —*Chu Ci* (Songs of the South), circa 300 BC,
> > tr. by David Hawkes

Dear Reader:

Before I can return your greeting, or
            pronounce farewell, I wish to offer you
the unique privilege of a preseason sale.

In order for you to participate,
I shall require the following information:
1) your name   2) your d.o.b.   3) your age   4) all your i.ds.
4) your user names   5) your codes   6) your passwords
7) your driving license   8) your employer   9) your street
address   10) your billing address   11) your shipping address
12) your Medicare number   13) your secondary insurance
number   14) All your tertiaries   15) your SSN   16) your
gender   17) your marital status   18) the number of your
children   19) all the above on spouse & infants as per 1-10
20) your c.i.a., your m.i.six, or k.g.b. i.d.s   21) your tempe-
rature   22) your blood pressure   23) Number of your pater-
nal granny's teeth   24) Number of your maternal granny's
teeth   25) Length of your penis if a male (in 16ths of an inch
por favor) or length of your vagina if a female (in 16ths
of an inch *por favor*)   26) your anal circumference
(in 16ths of an inch *por favor*)   27) your race or ethnic affi-
liation   28) your faith or lack of it   29) your education (gra-
duate only)   30) your *ism* if any   31) the date of your last prize,
and/or: award, review, encomium, bribe, or quid pro quo and/
or: all copulations for service rendered.

The above in triplicate or more if it please you.

In addition: 32) your best guess as to the date of
the achievement of universal lunacy   33) your best guess as to
the date of lattermost extinction   34) your best guess
as to the date of Exitus Generis Humani   35) your best guess
as to the devoration of this planet by the sun.

This survey is for the purpose of ensuring
that you receive all your benefits
and in no way is it designed to enrich us.

Your answers may be recorded
for technical or educational purposes and may be
hand delivered, e-mailed, texted, phoned, faxed, snail-mailed,
couriered or dumped (if not sent by passenger pigeon) to the
following address: "Asylum for the Hardly Rich & Minimally
Happy," Alt/Neue Mejiko, 87500.

Leave space for the development of future questions.
Do not forget to sign your bio-signature.
Please enjoy the last of this conversation
and have nice days.

i)

Where there is Mood. The sinkhole drops to pit of
the abyss which translates into Hades. The mood—
whatever can be said of it—begins to lighten. No
thing's as terrible as the true nightmare. The darkness
turns to shades of gray, life casts off the impossible:
not more, no never more than practice of the possible.
But a mind stumbles from one state to another. When
deep image is of a hanging bridge high over cliffs,
a neck caught in a noose high over cliffs. Though this
would sever vows and promises. How is it possible
this thing survival? No recognition on our part. Each
day warrants another day, the elevator takes mood up
and takes mood down while the desire to live and the
desire to die fail in reconciliation. Broken over abyss.
Pit deep. Friend said "It comes to all: do not invoke it."
(When arguing it would be best to leave, to disappear,
to fail to live the full of days allotted.) The heart no
longer anchored anywhere. Mind fails to recognize
its denizens, those that would once have manifested
lust to bones and sinews. A hesitation on a brink might
or might not design salvation. A lack of any appetite.
The prophets fail to see or apprehend their prophecy.
The sense that, day by day, one thought fails to con-
nect with all the other thoughts that *do* belong to it. Is
losing it. *It* mind you: it is losing *it*. *It* can no longer
apprehend the edge of things, tell edge from middle,
or from the break at which an edge desists. Fi-nal, End.

ii)

How terrible: the
count of people who do not exist. Who cannot prove
in any sense of mood to be alive. Yet are undead. And
what is then primarily their essence above all is to be
silent. That's so—they're silent. As the dying world
crumbles around them. Oh but their silence is excee-

ding loud! You hear no other noises as long as you're
on Earth. It breaks you down into the smallest shards.
Mood in its harshness fails to encompass you—as if
you could receive it even so! But, here and there, a
voice—not that loud kind of theirs, but like a deer's
entombed within a forest, a deer astonishingly rare:
no hunter's ever even seen it. Correction to the norm.
Faith is but a marinade known to the multitude as "Faith."
Religion's but belief in, oh, "Belief." The replication of
synanthropic species. You might, then almost say, on
target to extinction. Mood closes into theme and lasts.

iii)
Water. Flood cataracts inward, dictating all before it.
In poisoned oceans, whales at polluted krill: danger
of feasting. Now ice. Shatters to Thule's coruscations.
Bears drowning in white jackets without a necktie on.
Air. Pollution radiates around the globe. Birds choke
and children wretch in multi-million nests and cribs.
Earth. Mud slithers down hillsides over the indigent
from Aberfan to China. Fire. Forests never recorded
collapse on megaplans of future dwellings. National
borders swell in value as politicians swap their wealths.
Imperials buy patrimony in exotic lands to feed their
own home populations—exotics drown in famines.
Water flowing both ways blocked, suddenly arrested,
dam-circumscribed, shored up in altitudes. Down-
river others crave the water needed for their crops. It
is unending. Interminable. Insufferable. It continues.
And so: Let there be twenty times a year more floods
like these, fires like these, earthquakes like these. Let
migrants steal the ground under their feet, whole peo-
ples running from disaster to disaster. Vast populations
perish; millions of surplus newborns perish. Call on
the great crusades. *Any* crusades to catapult foul war.
Should humankind be on its way to the crimson planet:
even the giant Mars can be invoked among more recent
gods. The water wars—air, fire, all population wars:

let these erupt and flourish. Earth: open up your guts so
that whole armies sink in you yearning for mother love.
Let earth depopulate to space as remnants feed on roots.
And *you*? "I shall not willingly destroy this life, but *if*.
But if the final, ultimate, desires at me I'll not refuse."
Would you believe this as a hopeful cry to the awakened?